THE
Washington D.C.
EXPLORER'S
BUCKET LIST

Discover Washington D.C. Unforgettable Destinations and Create Lasting Memories! | Includes Washington Fun Facts, GPS coordinates & Travel Journal Log Section

Harris White

Disclaimer:

The information provided in The Washington D.C. Explorer's Bucket List, is intended for general informational purposes only. While every effort has been made to ensure the accuracy and reliability of the information contained within this travel guide, we cannot guarantee its completeness or timeliness.

Readers are advised to independently verify all details, including but not limited to, hours of operation, admission fees, transportation options, and availability of attractions and accommodations, before making any travel plans or decisions based on the information provided in this guide.

The inclusion of any specific destinations, attractions, accommodations, or services in this guide does not imply endorsement or recommendation by the publisher. Travelers are encouraged to exercise their own judgment and discretion when exploring Washington D.C. and to take appropriate precautions for their safety and well-being.

The publisher disclaim any liability for any loss, injury, or inconvenience sustained by individuals as a result of using the information presented in this travel guide. Travel at your own risk and enjoy the journey!

Table of Contents

INTRODUCTION

Welcome to the ultimate guide to exploring the wonders of Washington D.C.! Whether you're a seasoned traveler seeking new horizons or a wide-eyed wanderer embarking on your first journey, prepare to be captivated by the extraordinary diversity and boundless beauty of the Evergreen State. In this comprehensive guide, we invite you to embark on a thrilling odyssey through Washington's most iconic landmarks, hidden gems, and unforgettable experiences. Whether you're drawn to the towering peaks of the Cascade Mountains, the pristine waters of Puget Sound, or the vibrant tapestry of cultural riches woven throughout the region, Washington offers a bounty of treasures waiting to be uncovered. So, dust off your map, unleash your wanderlust, and prepare to check off your Washington Explorer's Bucket List one unforgettable experience at a time. From awe-inspiring natural wonders to thriving urban hubs, from adrenaline-fueled outdoor pursuits to soul-stirring cultural encounters, this guide is your passport to the myriad possibilities that await you in the Evergreen State. So, dear explorer, strap on your hiking boots, grab your camera, and prepare to embark on the journey of a lifetime. Whether you're scaling majestic peaks, kayaking through tranquil waters, or savoring the flavors of local cuisine, your Washington D.C. Explorer's Bucket List adventure awaits. Get ready to make memories that will last a lifetime and discover why Washington is truly a traveler's paradise.

HISTORY OF WASHINGTON

Washington State's history is full with the threads of indigenous cultures, European exploration, territorial disputes, and waves of migration. For thousands of years before European contact, the region was inhabited by diverse Native American tribes, each with its own languages, traditions, and territories. These tribes, including the Coast Salish, Chinook, Makah, and others, thrived on the abundant natural resources of the Pacific Northwest, relying on fishing, hunting, and gathering for sustenance.

The arrival of European explorers in the late 18th century marked a new chapter in Washington's history. Spanish explorer Juan Perez and British captain George Vancouver were among the first to chart the coast of what would become Washington State. In 1792, Vancouver claimed the region for Britain, while Spanish and American interests also laid claim to the territory. The resulting disputes over ownership and control eventually led to the Oregon Treaty of 1846, which established the boundary between British and American territory at the 49th parallel.

The mid-19th century brought a significant influx of settlers to the Pacific Northwest, spurred in part by the promise of fertile land and economic opportunity. The Oregon Trail, stretching from Missouri to the Oregon Territory, became the primary route for migrants seeking a better life in the West. In 1853, the Washington Territory was created, encompassing the lands west of the Cascade Range. This period of territorial expansion and settlement laid the groundwork for the development of Washington State as we know it today.

The late 19th and early 20th centuries witnessed rapid growth and industrialization in Washington, fueled by industries such as logging, mining, and agriculture. The arrival of the railroad in the late 19th century facilitated transportation and commerce, linking the region to markets across the country. Cities like Seattle and Tacoma emerged as bustling hubs of trade and industry, attracting immigrants from around the world seeking work and opportunity.

During this time, Washington also became a hotbed of progressive politics and social activism. Labor movements fought for workers' rights, leading to the establishment of labor laws and reforms. Figures like labor leader Mary Harris "Mother" Jones and socialist politician Eugene V. Debs played prominent roles in advocating for social justice and economic equality.

In the modern era, Washington has continued to evolve and thrive as a center of innovation and technology. Companies like Boeing, Microsoft, Amazon, and Starbucks have established themselves as global leaders in their respective industries, driving economic growth and prosperity in the region. Seattle, with its vibrant cultural scene, world-class museums, and progressive values, has become a magnet for artists, entrepreneurs, and forward-thinkers from around the world.

Today, Washington State remains a dynamic and diverse tapestry of cultures, landscapes, and experiences. From the towering peaks of the Cascade Range to the bustling streets of Seattle, the state's history and heritage are deeply intertwined with its natural beauty and urban sophistication. As Washington continues to chart its course into the 21st century, its rich history serves as a foundation for the challenges and opportunities that lie ahead.

WHY WASHINGTON FOR VACATION?

1. **Natural Beauty**: Washington is renowned for its breathtaking landscapes, ranging from the rugged coastline of the Pacific Ocean to the majestic peaks of the Cascade and Olympic mountain ranges. Visitors can explore lush rainforests, serene lakes, cascading waterfalls, and scenic national parks, providing endless opportunities for outdoor recreation and adventure.

2. **Outdoor Activities**: Whether you're into hiking, camping, skiing, kayaking, or whale watching, Washington has it all. With an abundance of trails, waterways, and outdoor spaces, adventurers of all skill levels can find activities to suit their interests and preferences year-round.

3. **Cultural Attractions**: From world-class museums and galleries to vibrant music venues and performing arts theaters, Washington offers a diverse array of cultural experiences. Explore Seattle's iconic Pike Place Market, visit the Museum of Pop Culture (MoPOP), or immerse yourself in Native American heritage at the Suquamish Museum.

4. **Food and Drink**: Washington's culinary scene is a gastronomic delight, featuring fresh seafood, locally sourced produce, and a thriving craft beer and wine culture. Indulge in Pacific Northwest specialties like salmon, oysters, and Dungeness crab, or embark on a tasting tour of the state's wineries and breweries.

5. **Urban Sophistication**: Seattle, Washington's largest city, boasts a vibrant urban landscape with world-class dining, shopping, and entertainment options. Explore the iconic Space Needle, stroll through historic neighborhoods like Pioneer Square, or take a ferry ride to nearby islands for a taste of Pacific Northwest island life.

6. **Family-Friendly Activities**: Washington offers plenty of family-friendly attractions and activities, including zoos, aquariums, amusement parks, and interactive museums. Whether you're exploring the hands-on exhibits at the Pacific Science Center or embarking on a wildlife safari at Northwest Trek Wildlife Park, there's no shortage of fun for the whole family.

7. **Scenic Drives and Road Trips**: Hit the road and explore Washington's scenic byways and winding mountain roads. From the breathtaking vistas of the North Cascades Highway to the charming small towns of the Olympic Peninsula, a road trip through Washington is a memorable way to experience the state's diverse landscapes and hidden gems.

8. **Year-Round Destination**: With four distinct seasons, Washington offers something for every traveler throughout the year. Whether you're skiing in the winter, hiking in the spring, kayaking in the summer, or admiring fall foliage in the autumn, there's never a bad time to visit the Evergreen State.

WASHINGTON MONUMENT: A BEACON OF FREEDOM IN THE NATION'S CAPITAL

Standing tall and proud in the center of the National Mall in Washington D.C., the Washington Monument is a national landmark honoring the country's first president, George Washington.

2 15th St NW, Washington, DC 20024, United States - +12024266841

Closest City/Town: Washington D.C.

Best Time to Visit: The monument is open year-round, but the best time to visit weather-wise is during the spring (March-May) or fall (September-November) when temperatures are mild.

Getting Around:

- **Metro:** The Washington Monument is easily accessible by Metro. Take the Blue, Orange, or Silver Line to the Smithsonian or Federal Triangle stations. Both stations are within walking distance of the monument.

- **Walking/Biking:** The National Mall is pedestrian and bike-friendly. You can explore the monument and surrounding memorials on foot or by renting a bike.

- **Driving:** While driving is an option, parking can be limited, especially during peak season. Consider using public transportation or ride-sharing services.

GPS Coordinates: 38° 53' 20″ N, 77° 00' 23″ W

Permit/Pass/Fees: Entry to the Washington Monument is free. However, obtaining a ticket in advance is recommended, especially during peak season. Tickets can be reserved online at https://www.nps.gov/wamo/planyourvisit/fees.htm.

Website: For more information on the Washington Monument, including hours of operation, accessibility options, and current events, visit the National Park Service website: https://www.nps.gov/wamo/

Fun Facts about the Washington Monument:

- Upon completion in 1884, it was the tallest building in the world for five years.

- The exterior is constructed of white marble, granite, and bluestone gneiss.

- The aluminum cap on the top was originally designed to be copper but was swapped due to weight concerns.
- An elevator takes visitors to the observation deck at the top, offering panoramic views of Washington D.C.

THE NATIONAL MALL: A SHOWCASE OF AMERICAN HISTORY AND CULTURE

The National Mall, a vast green space located in the heart of Washington D.C., is a must-visit destination for anyone interested in American history and culture. It stretches from the U.S. Capitol Building on the eastern end to the Lincoln Memorial on the western end, and is home to iconic monuments, museums, and memorials.

Washington, DC, United States - +12024266841

Closest City/Town: Washington D.C.

Best Time to Visit:

- The National Mall is open year-round, but the best time to visit weather-wise is during the spring (March-May) or fall (September-November) when temperatures are mild.

- Consider visiting during the National Cherry Blossom Festival in late March/early April for a truly spectacular experience.

Getting Around:

The National Mall is pedestrian-friendly and offers various ways to get around:

- **Walking/Biking:** The open space is perfect for exploring by foot or renting a bike.
- **Metro:** Several Metro stations border the National Mall. Take the Blue, Orange, or Silver Line to Smithsonian, Archives, Metro Center, or Capitol South stations.
- **Tram/Shuttle:** A free tram circles the National Mall, stopping at major attractions.

- **Driving:** While possible, parking can be limited and expensive, especially during peak seasons. Consider alternative methods of transportation.

GPS Coordinates: The National Mall is a large area, so coordinates will vary depending on your starting point. However, the U.S. Capitol Building (eastern end) is located at 38° 53′ 23″ N, 77° 00′ 27″ W, and the Lincoln Memorial (western end) is at 38° 53′ 20″ N, 77° 00′ 25″ W.

Permit/Pass/Fees: Most areas of the National Mall are free to access. However, some museums have entrance fees or require timed entry passes. It's recommended to check the websites of specific museums you plan to visit.

Website: For more information on the National Mall, including maps, transportation options, and a calendar of events, visit the National Park Service website: https://www.nps.gov/nama/

Fun Facts about the National Mall:

- Originally designed by Pierre Charles L'Enfant in 1791, the National Mall was envisioned as a "grand Avenue" for the nation's capital.

- The National Mall is home to over 100 monuments and memorials, including iconic structures like the Washington Monument, the Lincoln Memorial, and the Vietnam Veterans Memorial.

- The National Mall is also home to world-renowned Smithsonian Institution museums, such as the Air and Space Museum, the Natural History Museum, and the American History Museum.

- Each year, the National Mall attracts millions of visitors from around the world, making it one of the most popular tourist destinations in the United States.

WASHINGTON NATIONAL CATHEDRAL: A BEACON OF BEAUTY AND INSPIRATION

Towering over Washington D.C.'s northwest quadrant, the Washington National Cathedral is a majestic Gothic-style structure steeped in history and symbolism. More than just a house of worship, the cathedral serves as a place of inspiration, community, and national significance.

3101 Wisconsin Ave NW, Washington, DC 20016, United States - +12025376200

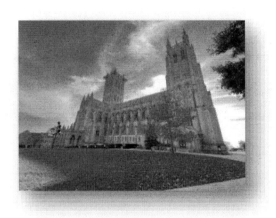

Closest City/Town: Washington D.C.

Best Time to Visit:

- The Washington National Cathedral is open year-round.

- Weekday mornings are generally less crowded than afternoons and weekends.

- Consider attending a worship service (free and open to the public) for a unique experience.

- During the holiday season, the cathedral comes alive with festive decorations and special events.

Getting Around:

- **Metro:** Take the Red Line to Cleveland Park or Van Ness-UDC stations. The cathedral is a short walk from either station.

- **Bus:** Several bus lines stop near the cathedral. Check WMATA (Washington Metropolitan Area Transit Authority) for route planning: https://buseta.wmata.com/

- **Driving:** Parking is available on-site for a fee, but can be limited. Consider alternative methods of transportation, especially during peak season.

GPS Coordinates: 38° 53′ 23″ N, 77° 00′ 32″ W

Permit/Pass/Fees:

- General admission tickets are required for self-guided tours.

- Docent-led tours are available for an additional fee.

- Some special events may have separate admission fees.

- Children under 4 are free.

Website: For current hours, ticket prices, and a calendar of events, visit the Washington National Cathedral website: https://cathedral.org/

Fun Facts about the Washington National Cathedral:

- Construction began in 1907 and wasn't completed until 1990, making it one of the longest construction projects in American history.

- Gargoyles and grotesques adorn the cathedral, each with a unique story or symbolism.

- Stained-glass windows throughout the cathedral depict biblical stories and historical figures.

- The cathedral has witnessed numerous historic events, including funeral services for presidents and religious leaders.

- At 328 feet (99 meters) tall, it is the second-largest church building in the United States and the tallest structure in Washington D.C. (excluding monuments).

THE LINCOLN MEMORIAL: A TRIBUTE TO A BELOVED PRESIDENT

Standing majestically at the western end of the National Mall in Washington D.C., the Lincoln Memorial is a national treasure that honors the legacy of President Abraham Lincoln. This iconic neoclassical monument serves as a powerful reminder of his leadership and the unifying spirit he embodied.

2 Lincoln Memorial Cir NW, Washington, DC 20002, United States - +12024266841

Closest City/Town: Washington D.C.

Best Time to Visit:

- The Lincoln Memorial is open year-round.

- Weekday mornings and evenings tend to be less crowded than afternoons and weekends.

- Consider visiting during spring (March-May) or fall (September-November) for pleasant weather.

Getting Around:

- **Metro:** Take the Blue, Orange, or Silver Line to Smithsonian or Metro Center stations. The memorial is within walking distance from either station.

- **Walking/Biking:** The National Mall is pedestrian and bike-friendly, making it easy to explore the Lincoln Memorial on foot or by renting a bike.

- **Driving:** While possible, parking can be limited, especially during peak season. Consider using public transportation or ride-sharing services.

GPS Coordinates: 38° 53′ 20″ N, 77° 00′ 23″ W

Permit/Pass/Fees: Entry to the Lincoln Memorial is free.

Website: For more information on the Lincoln Memorial, including hours of operation, accessibility options, and educational resources, visit the National Park Service website: https://www.nps.gov/places/000/lincoln-memorial.htm

Fun Facts about the Lincoln Memorial:

- Designed by Henry Bacon and completed in 1922, the memorial was inspired by the Parthenon in Athens, Greece.

- The interior features a 19-foot (5.8-meter) seated statue of Abraham Lincoln by Daniel Chester French.

- The words from Lincoln's Gettysburg Address are inscribed on the walls above the statue.

- The Lincoln Memorial has been the site of many historic speeches and rallies, including Martin Luther King Jr.'s iconic "I Have a Dream" speech in 1963.

- There are 36 Doric columns surrounding the monument, representing the number of states in the Union at the time of Lincoln's death.

WASHINGTON TRAVEL JOURNAL

Date: .... Transport: ....

Weather

Checklist For This Trip

Places:

Notes

Special Memories

SMITHSONIAN NATIONAL ZOOLOGICAL PARK

The Smithsonian National Zoological Park, also known as the National Zoo, is a haven for wildlife located in Washington D.C.'s Rock Creek Park. This free zoo is a popular destination for families and animal lovers, offering the opportunity to see a variety of fascinating creatures from around the globe.

3001 Connecticut Ave NW, Washington, DC 20008, United States - +12026334888

Closest City/Town: Washington D.C.

Best Time to Visit:

- The National Zoo is open year-round, but the spring (March-May) and fall (September-November) offer the most comfortable weather.

- Weekday mornings are generally less crowded than afternoons and weekends.

- Consider attending a special event or feeding time for a unique experience.

Getting Around:

- **Metro:** Take the Red Line to Woodley Park or Cleveland Park stations. The zoo is a short walk from either station.

- **Bus:** Several bus lines stop near the zoo entrance. Check WMATA (Washington Metropolitan Area Transit Authority) for route planning: https://buseta.wmata.com/

- **Car:** Parking is available on-site for a fee, but can be limited, especially during peak season. Consider alternative methods of transportation.

GPS Coordinates: 3001 Connecticut Ave NW, Washington, DC 20008 (38° 54′ 09″ N, 77° 01′ 23″ W)

Permit/Pass/Fees:

The National Zoo is free to enter, but advanced entry passes are required for all visitors, including infants. You can reserve your free passes online at [invalid URL removed]. While free, donations are always appreciated to support the zoo's mission.

Website: For more information on exhibits, animal encounters, events, and directions, visit the Smithsonian National Zoological Park website: https://nationalzoo.si.edu/

Fun Facts about the National Zoo:

- Founded in 1889, the National Zoo is one of the oldest zoos in the United States.

- The zoo is home to over 2,700 animals representing more than 390 species.

- The giant pandas are a popular attraction, and the zoo has been a leader in panda research and conservation for decades.

- The Asia Trail, featuring tigers, orangutans, and Komodo dragons, is a favorite among visitors.

- The National Zoo is committed to animal conservation and education, offering various programs and initiatives to inspire visitors.

INTERNATIONAL SPY MUSEUM, WASHINGTON D.C.

Calling all espionage enthusiasts! The International Spy Museum, located in Washington D.C.'s L'Enfant Plaza, is a thrilling and interactive museum that delves into the captivating world of spies and covert operations.

700 L'Enfant Plaza SW, Washington, DC 20024, United States - +12023937798

Closest City/Town: Washington D.C.

Best Time to Visit:

- The museum is open year-round. Weekdays tend to be less crowded than weekends, especially during peak tourist season.

- Consider visiting during the spring (March-May) or fall (September-November) for pleasant weather.

Getting Around:

- **Metro:** Take the Metro's Green, Yellow, or Silver Line to L'Enfant Plaza station. The museum is a short walk from the station.

- **Walking/Biking:** The museum is situated in a walkable area, and bike racks are available nearby.
- **Car:** Parking is available nearby for a fee, but can be limited. Consider ride-sharing services or public transportation.

GPS Coordinates: 700 L'Enfant Plaza SW, Washington, DC 20024 (38° 53′ 12″ N, 77° 00′ 22″ W)

Permit/Pass/Fees:

- Tickets are required for entry and can be purchased online in advance or on-site.
- Discounted rates are available for children, seniors, and military personnel.

Website: For current hours, ticket prices, exhibits, and special events, visit the International Spy Museum website: https://www.spymuseum.org/

Fun Facts about the International Spy Museum:

- Established in 2002, the International Spy Museum houses the largest collection of international espionage artifacts on public display.
- The museum offers interactive exhibits that allow visitors to test their spy skills in areas like code-breaking, disguise, and surveillance.
- The museum showcases real-life spy gadgets and tools used throughout history, from vintage cameras to miniature weapons.
- Visitors can learn about famous spies from different countries and eras, including ones from fiction like James Bond.
- The museum offers educational programs and workshops that delve deeper into the world of espionage and intelligence gathering.

WASHINGTON TRAVEL JOURNAL

Date: ....   Transport: ....

Weather	☁ ☀ 💧 🌙 ❄

Checklist For This Trip

Places:

Notes

Special Memories

UNITED STATES HOLOCAUST MEMORIAL MUSEUM, WASHINGTON D.C.

Standing as a solemn memorial to the victims of the Holocaust, the United States Holocaust Memorial Museum is a powerful and poignant museum located on the National Mall in Washington D.C. Through its exhibits and collections, the museum educates visitors on the horrors of the Holocaust and the importance of fighting against hatred and genocide.

100 Raoul Wallenberg Pl SW, Washington, DC 20024, United States - +12024880400

Closest City/Town: Washington D.C.

Best Time to Visit:

- The museum is open every day except Yom Kippur and Christmas Day.

- Weekdays tend to be less crowded than weekends, especially during peak tourist season.

- Allow ample time for your visit, as the museum is vast and the exhibits can be emotionally challenging.

Getting Around:

- **Metro:** Take the Metro's Blue, Orange, or Silver Line to Smithsonian or Metro Center stations. The museum is a short walk from either station.
- **Walking/Biking:** The museum is situated on the National Mall, which is pedestrian and bike-friendly.
- **Car:** Parking is available nearby for a fee, but can be limited. Consider ride-sharing services or public transportation.

GPS Coordinates: 100 Raoul Wallenberg Place SW, Washington, DC 20024 (38° 53′ 12″ N, 77° 00′ 27″ W)

Permit/Pass/Fees:

- Entry to the museum is free, but obtaining a timed pass online in advance is recommended, especially during peak seasons. You can reserve free passes at https://www.ushmm.org/information/visit-the-museum/plan-your-visit

- Donations are encouraged to support the museum's mission.

Website: For current hours, information on obtaining a timed pass, exhibits, and educational resources, visit the United States Holocaust Memorial Museum website: https://www.ushmm.org/

Fun Facts about the United States Holocaust Memorial Museum:

- Dedicated in 1993, the museum is the official memorial to the Holocaust in the United States.

- The museum houses a vast collection of artifacts, photographs, and testimonies that document the Holocaust.

- The permanent exhibition, titled "The Holocaust," takes visitors on a chronological journey through the events that led to and unfolded during the Holocaust.

- The museum serves as a powerful reminder of the dangers of unchecked hatred, prejudice, and indifference.

- Educational programs and resources are offered to promote tolerance, understanding, and civic responsibility.

UNITED STATES BOTANIC GARDEN, WASHINGTON D.C.

Situated on the grounds of the U.S. Capitol in Washington D.C., the United States Botanic Garden is a vibrant oasis showcasing an extensive collection of plants from around the world. This living museum serves as a center for education, conservation, and appreciation of the plant kingdom.

100 Maryland Ave SW, Washington, DC 20001, United States - +12022258333

Closest City/Town: Washington D.C.

Best Time to Visit:

- The Botanic Garden is open every day of the year, making it a flexible destination.

- Spring (March-May) offers a delightful display of blooming flowers, while fall (September-November) boasts vibrant foliage colors.

- Consider visiting during a special exhibit or event for a unique experience.

Getting Around:

- **Metro:** Take the Metro's Blue, Orange, or Silver Line to Capitol South station. The garden is a short walk from the station.

- **Walking/Biking:** The garden is situated near the National Mall, making it easily accessible on foot or by renting a bike.

- **Car:** Limited metered parking is available nearby. Consider ride-sharing services or public transportation, especially during peak season.

GPS Coordinates: 100 Maryland Ave SW, Washington, DC 20001 (38° 53′ 17″ N, 77° 00′ 47″ W)

Permit/Pass/Fees:

- Entry to the Conservatory and the National Garden is free.

- The Bartholdi Park, located across the street, is also free and open year-round.

Website: For current hours, information on exhibits, educational programs, and special events, visit the United States Botanic Garden website: https://www.usbg.gov/about-us

Fun Facts about the United States Botanic Garden:

- Established by Congress in 1820, it's one of the oldest continuously operating botanical gardens in the United States.

- The Conservatory houses a diverse collection of plants from various climate zones, including tropical rainforests, deserts, and Mediterranean gardens.

- The outdoor National Garden features seasonal displays of flowers, shrubs, and trees, showcasing the beauty of North American flora.

- The Botanic Garden offers educational programs and workshops for visitors of all ages, fostering appreciation for plants and their importance.

- Each year, the Botanic Garden hosts the popular "Season's Greenings" exhibit, featuring a magnificent indoor tree display and festive decorations.

UNITED STATES CAPITOL BUILDING, WASHINGTON D.C.

The United States Capitol Building, often simply referred to as the Capitol, is a majestic landmark towering over Washington D.C. It serves as the home of the United States Congress, the legislative branch of the federal government.

Washington, DC 20004, United States - +12022268000

Closest City/Town: Washington D.C.

Best Time to Visit:

• The Capitol is open to the public for tours most days, but schedules can vary depending on congressional sessions.

• Weekdays tend to be less crowded than weekends, especially during peak tourist season.

• Consider booking a guided tour in advance for a more in-depth experience.

Getting Around:

- **Metro:** Take the Metro's Red Line to Capitol South station or the Blue, Orange, or Silver Line to Union Station. The Capitol is within walking distance from either station.

- **Walking/Biking:** The Capitol is situated on Capitol Hill, which is pedestrian and bike-friendly.

- **Car:** Parking availability can be limited, especially during congressional sessions. Consider using public transportation or ride-sharing services.

GPS Coordinates: 38° 53′ 23″ N, 77° 00′ 27″ W

Permit/Pass/Fees:

- While free tours are sometimes offered, reservations are required and can fill up quickly.

- Free timed entry tickets for self-guided tours are also available and can be reserved online in advance: https://tours.visitthecapitol.gov/

Website: For current hours, information on booking tours, and accessibility options, visit the U.S. Capitol Visitor Center website: https://tours.visitthecapitol.gov/

Fun Facts about the United States Capitol:

- The cornerstone of the building was laid by President George Washington in 1793.

- The Capitol's dome, completed in 1866, is a recognizable symbol of the United States government.

- The building houses the Senate chamber and the House of Representatives chamber, where laws are debated and passed.

- The National Statuary Hall Collection features statues of prominent individuals from each state.

- The Capitol Rotunda, topped by a magnificent fresco, often serves as a backdrop for important national events.

SMITHSONIAN NATIONAL AIR AND SPACE MUSEUM, WASHINGTON D.C.

Embark on a celestial journey at the Smithsonian National Air and Space Museum (NASM) in Washington D.C. This is one of the largest and most popular museums dedicated to human flight and space exploration, igniting the imagination of visitors of all ages.

600 Independence Ave SW, Washington, DC 20560, United States - +12026332214

Closest City/Town: Washington D.C.

Best Time to Visit:

• The museum is open every day except for Christmas Day.

• Weekdays tend to be less crowded than weekends, especially during peak tourist season.

• Consider visiting during the spring (March-May) or fall (September-November) for pleasant weather.

- The museum undergoes renovations, so check their website for any temporary closures of specific exhibits.

Getting Around:

- **Metro:** Take the Metro's Blue, Orange, or Silver Line to L'Enfant Plaza or Smithsonian stations. The museum is within walking distance from either station.

- **Walking/Biking:** The National Mall, where the museum is located, is pedestrian and bike-friendly.

- **Car:** Parking can be limited, especially during peak season. Consider using public transportation or ride-sharing services.

GPS Coordinates: 600 Independence Ave SW, Washington, DC, 20560 (38° 53′ 20″ N, 77° 00′ 11″ W)

Permit/Pass/Fees:

- Entry to the main museum building on the National Mall is free.

- However, some special exhibitions may require a separate ticketed admission.

- Advanced timed entry reservations are recommended, especially during peak season. You can reserve free passes online at https://airandspace.si.edu/visit/museum-dc.

Website: For current hours, information on exhibits, educational programs, and special events, visit the Smithsonian National Air and Space Museum website: https://airandspace.si.edu/

Fun Facts about the Smithsonian National Air and Space Museum:

- Established in 1946, the NASM is a part of the Smithsonian Institution and houses the world's largest collection of aviation and space artifacts.

- Iconic exhibits include the Wright 1903 Flyer, the Apollo 11 command module, and the Space Shuttle Discovery (located at the Steven F. Udvar-Hazy Center in Virginia).

- The museum offers various educational programs, simulations, and flight experiences, making learning about air and space travel interactive and engaging.

- The museum constantly evolves with new exhibits, highlighting the latest advancements in aerospace technology and exploration.

- The NASM serves as a landmark of human innovation and a testament to our enduring fascination with the skies and beyond.

SMITHSONIAN NATIONAL MUSEUM OF NATURAL HISTORY, WASHINGTON D.C.

Delve into the captivating story of our planet at the Smithsonian National Museum of Natural History, located on the National Mall in Washington D.C. Nicknamed "America's attic" for its vast collections, this museum is a treasure trove for anyone interested in natural history, from dinosaurs to deep-sea creatures.

10th St. & Constitution Ave. NW, Washington, DC 20560, United States - +12026331000

Closest City/Town: Washington D.C.

Best Time to Visit:

- The museum is open every day except for December 25th.

- Weekdays tend to be less crowded than weekends, especially during peak tourist season.

- Spring (March-May) and fall (September-November) offer pleasant weather for exploring the National Mall.

Getting Around:

- **Metro:** Take the Metro's Blue, Orange, or Silver Line to Smithsonian or Metro Center stations. The museum is within walking distance from either station.

- **Walking/Biking:** The museum is situated on the National Mall, making it easily accessible on foot or by renting a bike.

- **Car:** Parking can be limited, especially during peak season. Consider using public transportation or ride-sharing services.

GPS Coordinates: 10th St & Constitution Ave NW, Washington, DC 20004 (38° 53′ 27″ N, 77° 00′ 12″ W)

Permit/Pass/Fees:

- Entry to the museum is free, but some special exhibits may require a separate ticketed admission.

- Free timed entry passes are recommended, especially during peak season. You can reserve passes online at https://naturalhistory.si.edu/visit.

Website: For current hours, information on exhibits, educational programs, and special events, visit the Smithsonian National Museum of Natural History website: https://naturalhistory.si.edu/

Fun Facts about the Smithsonian National Museum of Natural History:

- Established in 1910, it's one of the largest natural history museums in the world, housing over 146 million specimens.

- Iconic exhibits include the dinosaur hall featuring the T-Rex skeleton, the Hall of Human Origins exploring our evolutionary history, and the Giant Panda exhibit.

- The museum offers various educational programs, interactive displays, and tours, making science fun and engaging for visitors of all ages.

- Its extensive collections continue to be a resource for scientific research and discovery.

- The museum serves as a fascinating window into the natural world, inspiring wonder and curiosity about our planet's biodiversity and history.

WASHINGTON TRAVEL JOURNAL

Date: _____ Transport: _____

| Weather | ⛅ | ☀ | 💧 | 🌙 | ❄ |

Checklist For This Trip

_____

_____

_____

_____

_____

_____

_____

_____

_____

_____

_____

Special Memories

_____

_____

_____

_____

Places:

_____

_____

_____

_____

_____

_____

Notes

st

UNITED STATES NATIONAL ARBORETUM, WASHINGTON D.C.

The United States National Arboretum, situated in northeast Washington D.C., is a sprawling haven for plant enthusiasts. This 446-acre arboretum, administered by the U.S. Department of Agriculture, boasts a diverse collection of trees, shrubs, and flowers, offering a tranquil escape amidst the urban environment.

3501 New York Ave NE, Washington, DC 20002, United States - +12022452726

Closest City/Town: Washington D.C.

Best Time to Visit:

• The National Arboretum is open every day of the year except for Christmas Day.

• Spring (March-May) offers a vibrant display of blooming flowers, while fall (September-November) showcases a colorful foliage spectacle.

• Weekdays tend to be less crowded than weekends, especially during peak tourist season.

Getting Around:

- **Car:** The arboretum has two entrances: one at 3501 New York Avenue NE and the other at 24th & R Streets NE. Parking is available on-site, but it can be limited, especially during peak season.

- **Metro:** Take the Metro's Blue or Orange Line to Stadium Armory station. Transfer to bus B2 and exit at Bladensburg Road. While not the most direct route, it is an option for public transportation users.

GPS Coordinates: 3501 New York Ave NE, Washington, DC 20002 (38° 52′ 59″ N, 76° 59′ 07″ W)

Permit/Pass/Fees:

- Entry to the arboretum grounds is free.

- The National Bonsai & Penjing Museum located within the arboretum charges an admission fee. However, the museum is currently closed until further notice (as of March 23, 2024).

Website: For current hours, information on specific gardens and collections, and special events, visit the United States National Arboretum website: https://www.ars.usda.gov/northeast-area/washington-dc/national-arboretum/

Fun Facts about the United States National Arboretum:

- Established in 1927 by an act of Congress, the arboretum serves as a living museum for ornamental plants.

- It features a diverse collection of over 7,000 different types of plants, including bonsai trees, azaleas, camellias, and a National Grove of State Trees representing each U.S. state.

- The arboretum conducts research on plant breeding, disease resistance, and cultivation techniques, contributing to the advancement of horticulture.

- The arboretum offers educational programs and workshops throughout the year, fostering appreciation for plants and their environmental significance.

- The serene beauty of the arboretum provides a welcome respite from the city's hustle and bustle, making it a popular destination for nature enthusiasts and families alike.

THE THOMAS JEFFERSON MEMORIAL: A HOMAGE TO A FOUNDING FATHER

Standing majestically on the Tidal Basin in Washington D.C., the Thomas Jefferson Memorial is a tribute to the legacy of the third president of the United States. This neoclassical monument honors Jefferson's immense contributions to the nation, including his role as the principal author of the Declaration of Independence and his visionary ideals.

16 E Basin Dr SW, Washington, DC 20242, United States- +12024266841

Closest City/Town: Washington D.C.

Best Time to Visit:

- The memorial is open year-round, but the experience can vary depending on the season:

  o **Pleasant weather:** Spring (March-May) and fall (September-November) offer comfortable temperatures for exploring the grounds.

  o **Less crowded:** Weekdays tend to be less crowded than weekends, especially during peak tourist season.

  o **Cherry blossoms:** If you'd like to witness the iconic spectacle of blooming cherry trees surrounding the memorial, plan your visit for late March to early April (dates vary slightly each year).

Getting Around:

- **Metro:** Take the Metro's Blue, Orange, or Silver Line to Smithsonian station. The memorial is a short walk from the station (about 15 minutes).

- **Walking/Biking:** The National Mall, where the memorial is located, is pedestrian and bike-friendly. You can rent a bike for a scenic ride.

- **Car:** Parking can be limited, especially during peak season. Consider using public transportation, ride-sharing services, or biking if possible.

GPS Coordinates: 38° 53′ 20″ N, 77° 00′ 23″ W

Permit/Pass/Fees:

- Entry to the Thomas Jefferson Memorial is free.

Website: For current hours, information on accessibility options, and educational resources, visit the National Park Service website dedicated to the Thomas Jefferson Memorial: https://www.nps.gov/districtofcolumbia

Fun Facts about the Thomas Jefferson Memorial:

- Designed by John Russell Pope and completed in 1943, the monument draws inspiration from the Roman Pantheon.

- Inside the rotunda stands a 19-foot (5.8-meter) bronze statue of Thomas Jefferson by sculptor Daniel Chester French.

- The rotunda walls are inscribed with passages from Jefferson's most important writings, including the Declaration of Independence and the Virginia Statute for Religious Freedom.

- The 36 Doric columns surrounding the memorial represent the number of states in the Union at the time of Jefferson's death.

- The cherry blossom trees surrounding the basin were a gift from Japan in 1912, and the annual bloom signifies friendship between the two nations.

MERIDIAN HILL PARK (MALCOLM X PARK)

Meridian Hill Park, also known as Malcolm X Park, is a hidden gem located in the Columbia Heights and Adams Morgan neighborhoods of northwest Washington D.C. This 12-acre urban park offers a tranquil escape with its formal gardens, cascading fountains, and open green spaces.

16th St NW &, W St NW, Washington, DC 20009, United States - +12028956000

Closest City/Town: Washington D.C. (Columbia Heights & Adams Morgan neighborhoods)

Best Time to Visit:

- The park is open year-round, but the experience can vary depending on the season:

  o **Pleasant weather:** Spring (March-May) and fall (September-November) offer comfortable temperatures for enjoying the outdoors.

  o **Blooming flowers:** Spring offers vibrant displays of flowers, especially around the cascading fountain.

  o **Fewer crowds:** Weekdays tend to be less crowded than weekends, especially during peak tourist season.

Getting Around:

- **Metro:** Take the Metro's Green or Yellow Line to Columbia Heights station. The park is a short walk (about 10 minutes) from the station.

- **Bus:** Several bus lines stop near the park entrance. Check WMATA (Washington Metropolitan Area Transit Authority) for route planning: https://buseta.wmata.com/

- **Walking/Biking:** The park is easily accessible on foot or by bike.

- **Car:** Street parking is available in the surrounding neighborhoods, but it can be limited. Consider using public transportation or ride-sharing services.

GPS Coordinates: 16th & W Streets NW, Washington, DC 20001 (38° 54′ 12″ N, 77° 01′ 23″ W)

Permit/Pass/Fees:

- Entry to Meridian Hill Park is free.

Website: For information on park features, history, and events, you can visit the website of Washington Parks & People, a nonprofit organization that has partnered with the National Park Service in revitalizing the park: https://washingtonparks.net/about/

Fun Facts about Meridian Hill Park:

- Originally designed and built between 1912 and 1940, the park features a classical Italian Renaissance style with cascading fountains, symmetrical layouts, and a large reflecting pool.

- The park was named Meridian Hill because it sits on the exact longitude of the original District of Columbia milestone marker placed in 1791.

- In 1969, the park was unofficially co-named Malcolm X Park to honor the influential African American civil rights leader.

- The park has undergone restorations in recent years and is known as a safe and welcoming green space for the community.

- Visitors can enjoy picnics, walks, sports activities, or simply relax amidst the calming water features and formal gardens.

NATIONAL MUSEUM OF THE AMERICAN INDIAN, WASHINGTON D.C.

Immerse yourself in the rich tapestry of Native American cultures at the National Museum of the American Indian, situated on the National Mall in Washington D.C. This Smithsonian Institution museum is dedicated to showcasing the history, art, and traditions of Indigenous peoples from North, Central, and South America.

4th St SW, Washington, DC 20560, United States - +12026331000

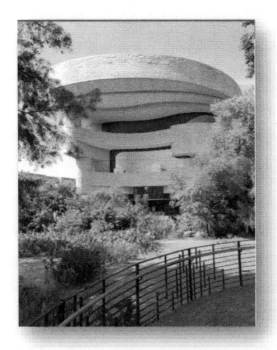

Closest City/Town: Washington D.C.

Best Time to Visit:

• The museum is open every day except for December 25th.

• Weekdays tend to be less crowded than weekends, especially during peak tourist season.

• Consider visiting during a special exhibit or event for a unique experience. Check the museum website for details.

Getting Around:

• **Metro:** Take the Metro's Blue, Orange, or Silver Line to L'Enfant Plaza station. The museum is a short walk from the station (about 10 minutes).

• **Walking/Biking:** The museum is situated on the National Mall, making it easily accessible on foot or by renting a bike.

• **Car:** Parking can be limited, especially during peak season. Consider using public transportation, ride-sharing services, or biking if possible.

GPS Coordinates: 4th Street & Independence Ave SW, Washington, DC 20001 (38° 53′ 12″ N, 77° 00′ 22″ W)

Permit/Pass/Fees:

• Entry to the museum is free.

Website: For current hours, information on exhibits, educational programs, and special events, visit the National Museum of the American Indian website: https://americanindian.si.edu/

Fun Facts about the National Museum of the American Indian:

• Established in 1989, it's the only national museum dedicated solely to the cultures of the Western Hemisphere's Indigenous peoples.

• The museum boasts a vast collection of over 800,000 objects, including textiles, pottery, jewelry, artwork, and everyday tools, offering a window into diverse tribal traditions.

- The museum's architectural design, with its emphasis on natural light and curving forms, reflects a collaborative effort with Native American tribes and communities.

- The museum offers a range of educational programs, films, and cultural demonstrations, fostering understanding and appreciation for Native American heritage.

- Visitors can explore permanent exhibits like "Our Journeys" and "Voices of Truth," or delve deeper into specific aspects of Native American culture through temporary exhibitions.

SMITHSONIAN NATIONAL MUSEUM OF AMERICAN INNOVATION, WASHINGTON D.C.

Explore the captivating story of the United States through its cultural artifacts and innovations at the Smithsonian National Museum of American History, located on Constitution Avenue NW in Washington, D.C. Often referred to as "America's attic," this museum is a treasure trove for anyone interested in American history, from everyday objects to groundbreaking inventions.

Closest City/Town: Washington D.C.

Best Time to Visit:

- The museum is open every day except for December 25th.

- Weekdays tend to be less crowded than weekends, especially during peak tourist season.

- Spring (March-May) and fall (September-November) offer pleasant weather for exploring the National Mall.

Getting Around:

- **Metro:** Take the Metro's Blue, Orange, or Silver Line to Smithsonian or Metro Center stations. The museum is within walking distance from either station (about a 10-minute walk).

- **Walking/Biking:** The museum is situated on the National Mall, making it easily accessible on foot or by renting a bike.

- **Car:** Parking can be limited, especially during peak season. Consider using public transportation, ride-sharing services, or biking if possible.

GPS Coordinates: 14th Street & Constitution Ave NW, Washington, DC 20056 (38° 53′ 27″ N, 77° 00′ 12″ W)

Permit/Pass/Fees:

- Entry to the museum is free, but some special exhibits may require a separate ticketed admission.

- Free timed entry passes are recommended, especially during peak season. You can reserve passes online at https://www.si.edu/.

Website: For current hours, information on exhibits, educational programs, and special events, visit the Smithsonian National Museum of American History website: https://www.si.edu/

Fun Facts about the Smithsonian National Museum of American History:

- Established in 1964, the museum houses over three million artifacts encompassing American social, political, cultural, scientific, and military history.

- Iconic exhibits include the Star-Spangled Banner, Dorothy's ruby slippers from the Wizard of Oz, and the Wright 1903 Flyer.

- The museum offers various educational programs, interactive displays, and demonstrations, bringing history to life for visitors of all ages.

- The museum's collections continue to grow, reflecting the ever-evolving story of the United States.

- It serves as a fascinating repository of American heritage, sparking curiosity and inspiring reflection on the nation's past, present, and future.

Washington Travel Journal

Date: .... Transport: ....

Weather	☁ ☀ 💧 🌙 ❄

Checklist For This Trip

Places:

Notes

Special Memories

NATIONAL PORTRAIT GALLERY, WASHINGTON D.C.

Standing on the National Mall in Washington D.C., the National Portrait Gallery showcases the captivating stories of America through portraits of iconic individuals. This Smithsonian Institution museum curates an impressive collection of paintings, sculptures, and photographs, all depicting figures who have shaped the nation's history and culture.

8th St NW & G St NW, Washington, DC 20001, United States - +12026338300

Closest City/Town: Washington D.C.

Best Time to Visit:

- The museum is open every day except for December 25th.

- Weekdays tend to be less crowded than weekends, especially during peak tourist season.

- Consider visiting during a special exhibit for a unique experience. Check the museum website for details.

Getting Around:

- **Metro:** Take the Metro's Blue, Orange, or Silver Line to Smithsonian or Metro Center stations. The museum is within walking distance from either station (about a 10-minute walk).

- **Walking/Biking:** The museum is situated on the National Mall, making it easily accessible on foot or by renting a bike.

- **Car:** Parking can be limited, especially during peak season. Consider using public transportation, ride-sharing services, or biking if possible.

GPS Coordinates: 8th and G Streets NW, Washington, DC 20001 (38° 53′ 12″ N, 77° 00′ 27″ W)

Permit/Pass/Fees:

- Entry to the museum is free.

Website: For current hours, information on exhibits, educational programs, and special events, visit the National Portrait Gallery website: https://npg.si.edu/home/national-portrait-gallery

Fun Facts about the National Portrait Gallery:

- Established in 1962 and opened to the public in 1968, it is the only complete collection of presidential portraits outside the White House.

- The museum's collection includes works by renowned artists like Gilbert Stuart, John Singer Sargent, and Chuck Close.

- Beyond presidents, the collection features portraits of poets, activists, inventors, scientists, and other figures who have left their mark on American society.

- The museum offers various educational programs, workshops, and tours, fostering appreciation for art and history.

- The National Portrait Gallery serves as a powerful reminder of the individuals who continue to shape the American story.

THE YARDS: A WATERFRONT DESTINATION IN WASHINGTON D.C.

The Yards is a captivating waterfront development revitalizing Washington D.C.'s Navy Yard neighborhood. This 42-acre destination seamlessly blends modern urban living with historic charm, offering a vibrant mix of residential spaces, shops, restaurants, entertainment, and green spaces.

1300 First St SE, Washington, DC 20003, United States

Closest City/Town: Washington D.C.

Best Time to Visit:

- The Yards is a year-round destination.

- Spring (March-May) and fall (September-November) offer pleasant weather for outdoor activities like enjoying the waterfront park.

- Summer (June-August) can be hot and humid, but there are plenty of indoor options like shops and restaurants.

- Weekdays tend to be less crowded than weekends, especially during peak tourist season.

- Consider special events happening at The Yards or nearby Nationals Park for a unique experience. Check their website for details: https://twitter.com/TheYardsDC

Getting Around:

- **Metro:** Take the Metro's Green Line to Waterfront station. The Yards is within walking distance (about 10 minutes).

- **Walking/Biking:** The Yards is pedestrian and bike-friendly, making it easy to explore on foot or by renting a bike.

- **Car:** Parking can be limited, especially during events or peak season. Consider using public transportation, ride-sharing services, or biking if possible.

- **Water Taxi:** During warmer months, consider using the DC Water Taxi for a scenic ride to The Yards from other waterfront areas like Georgetown or National Harbor.

GPS Coordinates: 38° 53′ 23″ N, 77° 00′ 27″ W (This is the center point of The Yards development.)

Permit/Pass/Fees:

- There is no general fee to enter The Yards.

- Parking fees may apply depending on the chosen method and duration.

- Some events or activities within The Yards may have separate admission fees.

Website: For current hours, a directory of shops and restaurants, upcoming events, and information on getting around, visit The Yards website: https://twitter.com/TheYardsDC

Fun Facts about The Yards:

- The Yards incorporates revitalized historic buildings alongside modern architecture, creating a unique blend of old and new.

- The centerpiece of The Yards is the award-winning Yards Park, a popular spot for relaxing, enjoying waterfront views, and attending seasonal events.

- The Yards Marina offers boat slips for residents and is a starting point for exploring the Anacostia River by water.

- The Yards is home to the Thompson Hotel, a luxury hotel with stunning river views.

- Nationals Park, home to the Washington Nationals baseball team, is located just steps away from The Yards, making it a great spot to catch a game and enjoy the surrounding entertainment district.

NATIONAL MUSEUM OF AFRICAN AMERICAN HISTORY AND CULTURE, WASHINGTON D.C.

Steeped in history and brimming with culture, the National Museum of African American History and Culture (NMAAHC) stands proudly on the National Mall in Washington D.C. This Smithsonian Institution museum serves as a national treasure, chronicling the experiences of African Americans from slavery to the present day.

1400 Constitution Ave. NW, Washington, DC 20560, United States - +18447503012

Closest City/Town: Washington D.C.

Best Time to Visit:

- The museum is open every day except for December 25th.

- Weekdays tend to be less crowded than weekends, especially during peak tourist season.

- Due to the museum's popularity, it's highly recommended to reserve free timed entry passes in advance, particularly during peak times. You can do so online at https://nmaahc.si.edu/visit/plan-your-visit.

Getting Around:

- **Metro:** Take the Metro's Blue, Orange, or Silver Line to Smithsonian or Metro Center stations. The museum is within walking distance from either station (about a 10-minute walk).

- **Walking/Biking:** The museum is situated on the National Mall, making it easily accessible on foot or by renting a bike.

- **Car:** Parking can be limited, especially during peak season. Consider using public transportation, ride-sharing services, or biking if possible.

GPS Coordinates: 14th Street & Constitution Ave NW, Washington, DC 20056 (38° 53′ 27″ N, 77° 00′ 12″ W)

Permit/Pass/Fees:

- Entry to the museum is free, but some special exhibits may require a separate ticketed admission.

Website: For current hours, information on exhibits, educational programs, and special events, visit the National Museum of African American History and Culture website: https://nmaahc.si.edu/visit/plan-your-visit

Fun Facts about the National Museum of African American History and Culture:

- Established in 2003 and opened in 2016, it's the only national museum solely dedicated to the documentation of African American life, history, and culture.

- The museum's striking bronze-colored exterior pays homage to the intricate ironwork crafted by enslaved African Americans.

- The NMAAHC houses more than 40,000 objects, with exhibits exploring everything from slavery and segregation to art, music, and social movements.

- Interactive displays and educational programs bring history to life for visitors of all ages.

- The museum serves as a powerful testament to the resilience, creativity, and contributions of African Americans throughout U.S. history.

WASHINGTON TRAVEL JOURNAL

Date: ....   Transport: ....

Weather

Checklist For This Trip

Places:

Notes

Special Memories

NATIONAL GALLERY OF ART, WASHINGTON D.C.: A TREASURE TROVE OF WESTERN ART

Standing majestically on the National Mall in Washington D.C., the National Gallery of Art is a haven for art enthusiasts. This prestigious museum, administered by the U.S. Department of Agriculture, boasts a vast collection of paintings, sculptures, prints, and decorative arts, spanning centuries and continents.

Constitution Ave. NW, Washington, DC 20565, United States - +12027374215

Closest City/Town: Washington D.C.

Best Time to Visit:

- The National Gallery of Art is open daily from 10:00 a.m. to 5:00 p.m. and is closed on December 25th and January 1st.

- Weekdays tend to be less crowded than weekends, especially during peak tourist season.

- Spring (March-May) and fall (September-November) offer pleasant weather for exploring the National Mall.

Getting Around:

- **Metro:** Take the Metro's Blue or Orange Line to Smithsonian station. The National Gallery is a short walk from the station (about 10 minutes).

- **Walking/Biking:** The National Gallery is situated on the National Mall, making it easily accessible on foot or by renting a bike.

- **Car:** Parking can be limited, especially during peak season. Consider using public transportation, ride-sharing services, or biking if possible.

GPS Coordinates: * West Building: 6th St and Constitution Ave NW, Washington, DC 20001 (38° 53' 40" N, 77° 00' 10" W) * East Building: 4th St and Constitution Ave NW, Washington, DC 20001 (38° 53' 27" N, 77° 00' 12" W)

Permit/Pass/Fees:

- Entry to the National Gallery of Art is free.

- Special exhibits may have a separate admission fee.

Website: For current hours, information on exhibits, educational programs, and special events, visit the National Gallery of Art website: https://www.nga.gov/

Fun Facts about the National Gallery of Art:

- Established in 1937 through a joint resolution of the U.S. Congress, the National Gallery of Art houses works donated by private collectors like Andrew W. Mellon and Ailsa Mellon Bruce.

- The Gallery's collection encompasses over 141,000 works of art, tracing the development of Western art from the Middle Ages to the present day.

- It includes iconic pieces like Leonardo da Vinci's "Ginevra de' Benci," the only painting by the artist in the Americas, and Vincent van Gogh's "Sunflowers."

- The National Gallery offers a variety of educational programs, tours, lectures, and films throughout the year.

- The serene beauty of the National Gallery and its expansive collection provide a captivating art experience for visitors worldwide.

THE KOREAN WAR VETERANS MEMORIAL, WASHINGTON D.C.

The Korean War Veterans Memorial stands proudly in West Potomac Park, Washington D.C., southeast of the Lincoln Memorial. This poignant memorial commemorates the brave American soldiers who served in the Korean War (1950-1953).

900 Ohio Dr SW, Washington, DC 20024, United States - +12024266841

Closest City/Town: Washington D.C.

Best Time to Visit:

• The memorial is open 24 hours a day, year-round.

• Consider visiting during daylight hours for the best views and lighting for photos.

• Weekdays tend to be less crowded than weekends, especially during peak tourist season.

Getting Around:

- **Metro:** Take the Metro's Blue or Orange Line to Smithsonian station. The memorial is a short walk from the station (about 15 minutes).

- **Walking/Biking:** The memorial is situated near the National Mall, making it easily accessible on foot or by renting a bike.

- **Car:** Parking can be limited, especially during peak season. Consider using public transportation, ride-sharing services, or biking if possible.

GPS Coordinates: 38° 53′ 22″ N, 77° 02′ 09″ W

Permit/Pass/Fees:

- There is no entrance fee to visit the Korean War Veterans Memorial.

Website: For information on the memorial's history, maintenance, and accessibility, visit the American Battle Monuments Commission website: https://www.abmc.gov/

Fun Facts about the Korean War Veterans Memorial:

- Dedicated in 1995, the memorial features 19 stainless steel statues depicting soldiers from all branches of the U.S. military service in realistic combat poses.

- A granite memorial wall, added in 2022, honors the over 36,000 American service members who died in the war, along with over 7,200 members of the Korean Augmentation to the U.S. Army.

- The triangular-shaped memorial wall resembles a battlefield map, with the stainless steel figures standing guard.

- A reflecting pool in front of the statues creates a contemplative atmosphere, allowing visitors to reflect on the sacrifices made during the Korean War.

- The Korean War Veterans Memorial serves as a powerful tribute to the courage and dedication of the American service members who fought in this often-overlooked conflict.

TUDOR PLACE HISTORIC HOUSE & GARDEN: A GEORGETOWN GEM

Tudor Place, situated on a full city block in the heart of Georgetown, Washington D.C., is a captivating historic house museum. This Federal-style mansion, originally built for Martha Parke Custis Peter and her husband Thomas Peter, offers a glimpse into the lives of prominent residents from the early 19th century to the 20th century.

1644 31st St NW, Washington, DC 20007, United States - +12029650400

Closest City/Town: Washington D.C. (Georgetown neighborhood)

Best Time to Visit:

• Tudor Place is open for self-guided tours Saturdays and Sundays from noon to 4 pm.

• Advanced reservations are required and can be made online at https://tudorplace.org/.

• Spring (March-May) and fall (September-November) offer pleasant weather for exploring the gardens.

• Weekends are the only days the house is open to the public, so expect more crowds then.

Getting Around:

• **Metro:** Take the Metro's Blue, Orange, or Silver Line to Foggy Bottom station. From there, it's a 1-mile walk or a short ride-sharing service trip to Tudor Place.

• **Walking/Biking:** The property is situated in Georgetown, a walkable neighborhood. Bikes can be rented for exploring the area.

• **Car:** Street parking can be limited, especially on weekends. Consider using public transportation, ride-sharing services, or biking if possible.

GPS Coordinates: 1644 31st Street NW, Washington, DC 20007 (38° 53′ 20″ N, 77° 00′ 23″ W)

Permit/Pass/Fees:

• Admission tickets are required and can be purchased online in advance: https://tudorplace.org/

• Docent-led tours are available for an additional fee.

Website: For current hours, information on tours, tickets, and the property's history, visit the Tudor Place Historic House & Garden website: https://tudorplace.org/

Fun Facts about Tudor Place:

- Constructed around 1794 and completed by 1815, Tudor Place is one of the few remaining early-19th-century estate homes in the nation's capital with its surrounding landscape largely intact.

- The house belonged to six generations of Martha Washington's descendants, who lived there from 1805 to 1983.

- Tudor Place was not only a home but also a working plantation, with enslaved people who toiled to maintain the property. The site acknowledges this complex history through exhibits and educational programs.

- The property boasts over 18,000 decorative objects, including the largest collection of George Washington memorabilia outside of Mount Vernon.

- Tudor Place's beautiful gardens showcase period-appropriate landscaping and offer a serene escape in the heart of the city.

VIETNAM VETERANS MEMORIAL, WASHINGTON D.C.

Standing tall on the National Mall in Washington D.C., the Vietnam Veterans Memorial is a poignant tribute to the men and women who served in the Vietnam War (1955-1975). This powerful memorial honors those who died or remain missing in action during the conflict.

5 Henry Bacon Dr NW, Washington, DC 20002, United States - +12024266841

Closest City/Town: Washington D.C.

Best Time to Visit:

- The memorial is open 24 hours a day, year-round.

- Consider visiting during daylight hours for the best views and lighting for photos.

- Weekdays tend to be less crowded than weekends, especially during peak tourist season.

Getting Around:

- **Metro:** Take the Metro's Blue or Orange Line to Smithsonian station. The memorial is a short walk from the station (about 10 minutes).

- **Walking/Biking:** The memorial is situated on the National Mall, making it easily accessible on foot or by renting a bike.

- **Car:** Parking can be limited, especially during peak season. Consider using public transportation, ride-sharing services, or biking if possible.

GPS Coordinates: 5 Lincoln Memorial Dr NW, Washington, DC 20037 (38° 53' 22" N, 77° 00' 25" W)

Permit/Pass/Fees:

- There is no entrance fee to visit the Vietnam Veterans Memorial.

Website: For information on the memorial's history, symbolism, and educational resources, visit the National Park Service website: https://www.nps.gov/vive/

Fun Facts about the Vietnam Veterans Memorial:

- Designed by Maya Lin, a young Yale University student, the memorial consists of two black granite walls, V-shaped, inscribed with the names of over 58,000 American service members.

- The names are listed chronologically, by date of casualty, creating a powerful sense of time and loss.

- Visitors are often seen leaving mementos, letters, or flags at the wall, creating a personal and moving experience.

- The Vietnam Veterans Memorial Wall is a powerful symbol of the human cost of war and serves as a place for reflection, healing, and remembrance.

- In addition to the main memorial wall, the complex also includes the Three Soldiers statue, a bronze sculpture depicting three servicemen, and the Vietnam Women's Memorial, honoring the women who served during the war.

Washington Travel Journal

Date: ....   Transport: ....

Weather	☁ ☀ 💧 🌙 ❄

Checklist For This Trip

Places:

Special Memories

Notes

NATIONAL BUILDING MUSEUM, WASHINGTON D.C.

The National Building Museum, situated in the heart of Washington D.C.'s historic Judiciary Square neighborhood, is a captivating institution dedicated to the history and impact of the built environment. This museum, a former pension bureau building, boasts grand architecture and houses a diverse collection of exhibits exploring architecture, design, engineering, construction, and urban planning.

401 F St NW, Washington, DC 20001, United States - +12022722448

Closest City/Town: Washington D.C.

Best Time to Visit:

• The museum is open every day except for December 25th.

• Weekdays tend to be less crowded than weekends, especially during peak tourist season.

• Consider visiting during a special exhibit or event for a unique experience. Check the museum website for details: https://www.nbm.org/

Getting Around:

- **Metro:** Take the Metro's Blue, Orange, or Silver Line to Judiciary Square station. The museum is directly adjacent to the station.

- **Walking/Biking:** The museum is easily accessible on foot or by renting a bike, being situated near the National Mall.

- **Car:** Parking can be limited, especially during peak season. Consider using public transportation, ride-sharing services, or biking if possible.

GPS Coordinates: 401 F St NW, Washington, DC 20001 (38° 53′ 12″ N, 77° 00′ 22″ W)

Permit/Pass/Fees:

- Entry to the museum's permanent collection is free.

- Special exhibits may require a separate ticketed admission.

Website: For current hours, information on exhibits, educational programs, and special events, visit the National Building Museum website: https://www.nbm.org/

Fun Facts about the National Building Museum:

- Established in 1980, it's the only institution in the United States solely dedicated to exploring the history and impact of architecture, engineering, and design.

- The museum is housed in a magnificent Romanesque Revival building completed in 1887, designed by Montgomery C. Meigs, the U.S. Army quartermaster general.

- The National Building Museum boasts a vast collection of artifacts, including architectural models, building materials, tools, and objects that illuminate the evolution of construction and design.

- Interactive exhibits and educational programs bring the built environment to life for visitors of all ages.

- The museum's grand hall, with its soaring columns and expansive space, is a sight to behold in itself and often serves as a venue for events and exhibitions.

SMITHSONIAN AMERICAN ART MUSEUM: UNVEILING AMERICA'S STORY THROUGH ART

Explore the captivating story of the United States through its cultural artifacts and innovations at the Smithsonian American Art Museum, located on Constitution Avenue NW in Washington, D.C. Often referred to as "America's attic," this museum is a treasure trove for anyone interested in American history, from everyday objects to groundbreaking inventions.

G Street Northwest &, 8th St NW, Washington, DC 20004, United States - +12026331000

Closest City/Town: Washington D.C.

Best Time to Visit:

- The museum is open every day except for December 25th.

- Weekdays tend to be less crowded than weekends, especially during peak tourist season.

- Spring (March-May) and fall (September-November) offer pleasant weather for exploring the National Mall.

Getting Around:

- **Metro:** Take the Metro's Blue, Orange, or Silver Line to Smithsonian or Metro Center stations. The museum is within walking distance from either station (about a 10-minute walk).

- **Walking/Biking:** The museum is situated on the National Mall, making it easily accessible on foot or by renting a bike.

- **Car:** Parking can be limited, especially during peak season. Consider using public transportation, ride-sharing services, or biking if possible.

GPS Coordinates: 14th Street & Constitution Ave NW, Washington, DC 20056 (38° 53′ 27″ N, 77° 00′ 12″ W)

Permit/Pass/Fees:

- Entry to the museum is free, but some special exhibits may require a separate ticketed admission.

- Free timed entry passes are recommended, especially during peak season. You can reserve passes online at https://americanart.si.edu/.

Website: For current hours, information on exhibits, educational programs, and special events, visit the Smithsonian American Art Museum website: https://americanart.si.edu/

Fun Facts about the Smithsonian American Art Museum:

- Established in 1964, the museum houses over three million artifacts encompassing American social, political, cultural, scientific, and military history.

- Iconic exhibits include the Star-Spangled Banner, Dorothy's ruby slippers from the Wizard of Oz, and the Wright 1903 Flyer.

- The museum offers various educational programs, interactive displays, and demonstrations, bringing history to life for visitors of all ages.

- The museum's collections continue to grow, reflecting the ever-evolving story of the United States.

- It serves as a fascinating repository of American heritage, sparking curiosity and inspiring reflection on the nation's past, present, and future.

DUMBARTON OAKS MUSEUM, WASHINGTON D.C.

Situated in the Georgetown neighborhood of Washington D.C., Dumbarton Oaks Museum is a hidden gem for art and history enthusiasts. This historic estate, originally a residence and gardens, now houses an impressive collection of Byzantine and Pre-Columbian art alongside European decorative arts and medieval and Renaissance works.

1703 32nd St NW, Washington, DC 20007, United States - +12023396400

Closest City/Town: Washington D.C. (Georgetown neighborhood)

Best Time to Visit:

• The museum is open Tuesday through Sunday, from 11:30 am to 5:30 pm.

• Weekdays tend to be less crowded than weekends, especially during peak tourist season.

• Spring (March-May) and fall (September-November) offer pleasant weather for exploring the gardens, a highlight of the estate.

Getting Around:

- **Metro:** Take the Metro's Blue or Orange Line to Foggy Bottom station. From there, it's a 1-mile walk or a short ride-sharing service trip to Dumbarton Oaks.
- **Walking/Biking:** The museum is situated in Georgetown, a walkable neighborhood. Bikes can be rented for exploring the area.
- **Car:** Street parking can be limited, especially on weekends. Consider using public transportation, ride-sharing services, or biking if possible.

GPS Coordinates: 1703 32nd St NW, Washington, DC 20007 (38° 53′ 09″ N, 77° 00′ 27″ W)

Permit/Pass/Fees:

- Admission fees apply for both the museum and gardens. You can purchase tickets online in advance: http://museum.doaks.org/
- Docent-led tours are available for an additional fee.

Website: For current hours, information on exhibits, educational programs, and special events, visit the Dumbarton Oaks Museum website: http://museum.doaks.org/

Fun Facts about Dumbarton Oaks Museum:

- Founded in 1940 by wealthy philanthropists Robert Woods Bliss and Mildred Barnes Bliss, the estate and its collections were gifted to Harvard University.

- The museum's Byzantine collection is one of the most significant in North America, spanning the imperial, ecclesiastical, and secular realms from the 4th to 15th centuries.

- The Pre-Columbian collection offers a glimpse into the artistic achievements of ancient Mesoamerican and Andean civilizations.

- The beautifully landscaped gardens, designed by Beatrix Farrand, are a masterpiece of horticultural design and integrate seamlessly with the museum buildings.

- Dumbarton Oaks Museum serves as a unique center for scholarly research, public education, and the appreciation of art, history, and horticulture.

WASHINGTON TRAVEL JOURNAL

Date: _____   Transport: _____

Weather	☁️ ☀️ 💧 🌙 ❄️

Checklist For This Trip

Places:

Special Memories

Notes

FREDERICK DOUGLASS NATIONAL HISTORIC SITE, WASHINGTON D.C.

Steeped in history and brimming with the spirit of activism, the Frederick Douglass National Historic Site stands proudly in Anacostia, a neighborhood east of the Anacostia River in Washington D.C. This national park site encompasses the last home of Frederick Douglass, a pivotal figure in the abolitionist movement, writer, orator, statesman, and champion of human rights.

1411 W St SE, Washington, DC 20020, United States - 1411 W St SE, Washington, DC 20020, United States

Closest City/Town: Washington D.C. (Anacostia neighborhood)

Best Time to Visit:

• The historic house is open for tours Tuesdays through Sundays, from 9 am to 5 pm (April 15 - October 15) and 9 am to 4 pm (October 16 - April 14).

• Weekdays tend to be less crowded than weekends, especially during peak tourist season.

• Reservations are required for groups of 10 or more. You can check for current hours and make reservations online at the National Park Service website (https://www.nps.gov/frdo/).

Getting Around:

- **Metro:** Take the Metro's Blue, Orange, or Silver Line to Anacostia station. From there, it's a 1-mile walk or a short ride-sharing service trip to the site.

- **Bus:** Several Metrobus lines stop near the Frederick Douglass National Historic Site.

- **Car:** Parking is available on-site, but it can be limited, especially during peak season. Consider using public transportation, ride-sharing services, or biking if possible.

GPS Coordinates: 1411 W Street, SE, Washington, DC 20056 (38° 53′ 18″ N, 77° 00′ 07″ W)

Permit/Pass/Fees:

- Entrance to the grounds is free.

- There is no entrance fee for the self-guided tour of the house museum, but donations are gratefully accepted.

- Ranger-led tours are offered for a nominal fee.

Website: For current hours, information on tours, educational programs, and the history of the site, visit the National Park Service website: https://www.nps.gov/frdo/

Fun Facts about the Frederick Douglass National Historic Site:

- Established in 1988, the site preserves Cedar Hill, the home Douglass purchased in 1877 and lived in until his death in 1895.

- The house offers a glimpse into Douglass's life as a writer, intellectual, and political leader.

- The site also includes a reconstructed greenhouse, reflecting Douglass's interest in horticulture.

- The Frederick Douglass National Historic Site serves as a powerful testament to the enduring legacy of this remarkable figure who fought tirelessly for equality and justice.

Certainly! Here's the information about Hillwood Estate, Museum & Gardens, Washington D.C.:

HILLWOOD ESTATE, MUSEUM & GARDENS

Located in northwest Washington D.C., Hillwood Estate, Museum & Gardens offers a captivating glimpse into the life and collections of Marjorie Merriweather Post, a prominent socialite and businesswoman. This grand estate, now a museum, showcases stunning French decorative arts, exquisite Russian imperial art, and serene formal gardens.

4155 Linnean Ave NW, Washington, DC 20008, United States - +12026865807

Closest City/Town: Washington D.C.

Best Time to Visit:

- Hillwood is open Wednesday through Sunday, from 10:00 am to 5:00 pm.

- Closed Mondays and Tuesdays, and on Thanksgiving Day and Christmas Day.

- Weekdays tend to be less crowded than weekends, especially during peak tourist season.

- Spring (March-May) and fall (September-November) offer pleasant weather for exploring the gardens.

Getting Around:

- **Metro:** Take the Metro's Red Line to Cleveland Park station. From there, it's a 1.5-mile walk, a short bus ride, or a ride-sharing service trip to Hillwood.

- **Bus:** Several Metrobus lines stop near the estate.

- **Car:** Parking is available on-site, but it can be limited, especially during peak season. Consider using public transportation, ride-sharing services, or biking if possible.

GPS Coordinates: 2600 Foxhall Rd NW, Washington, DC 20007 (38° 54′ 12″ N, 77° 04′ 22″ W)

Permit/Pass/Fees:

- Admission fees apply and can be purchased online in advance: https://hillwoodmuseum.org/visit/hours-tickets.

- Free timed entry passes are recommended, especially during peak season.

Website: For current hours, information on exhibits, educational programs, and special events, visit the Hillwood Estate, Museum & Gardens website: https://hillwoodmuseum.org/visit/hours-tickets

Fun Facts about Hillwood Estate, Museum & Gardens:

- Built in the 1920s by Marjorie Merriweather Post, Hillwood was designed to house her vast collection of art and treasures.

- The mansion boasts opulent interiors decorated with French decorative arts, tapestries, and furniture.

- Hillwood's collection of Russian imperial art is one of the most comprehensive outside of Russia, featuring Fabergé eggs, paintings, and jewelry.

- The estate encompasses thirteen acres of beautifully landscaped formal gardens, including a French parterre, a Japanese-style garden, and a rose garden.

- Hillwood Estate, Museum & Gardens serves as a fascinating portal into the world of a bygone era, showcasing art, history, and the life of a remarkable collector.

THE LINCOLN MEMORIAL REFLECTING POOL, WASHINGTON D.C.

Situated on the National Mall in Washington D.C., the Lincoln Memorial Reflecting Pool stretches majestically between the Lincoln Memorial and the Washington Monument. This rectangular pool serves not only as a visual complement to the iconic monuments but also offers a tranquil space for reflection.

2 Lincoln Memorial Cir NW, Washington, DC 20024, United States - +12024266841

Closest City/Town: Washington D.C.

Best Time to Visit:

• The reflecting pool is accessible 24 hours a day, year-round.

• Consider visiting during daylight hours for the best views and for capturing reflections in the pool.

• Weekdays tend to be less crowded than weekends, especially during peak tourist season.

Getting Around:

• **Metro:** Take the Metro's Blue or Orange Line to Smithsonian station. The reflecting pool is a short walk from the station (about 15 minutes).

- **Walking/Biking:** The reflecting pool is situated near the National Mall, making it easily accessible on foot or by renting a bike.

- **Car:** Parking can be limited, especially during peak season. Consider using public transportation, ride-sharing services, or biking if possible.

GPS Coordinates: 38° 53′ 24″ N, 77° 02′ 11″ W (Located between the Lincoln Memorial and Washington Monument)

Permit/Pass/Fees:

- There is no entrance fee to visit the Lincoln Memorial Reflecting Pool.

Website:

- For information on the National Mall and surrounding memorials, visit the National Park Service website: https://www.nps.gov/nama/

Fun Facts about the Lincoln Memorial Reflecting Pool:

- Designed by architect Henry Bacon, the reflecting pool was constructed in 1922 and 1923, following the dedication of the Lincoln Memorial.

- At nearly 2,030 feet long and 167 feet wide, it's one of the largest reflecting pools in the United States.

- The pool's depth ranges from 18 inches at the edges to 30 inches in the center.

- Originally filled with Washington D.C.'s drinking water, the pool's circulation system was later updated to use a sustainable water source from the Tidal Basin, reducing water consumption.

- The reflecting pool's calm surface creates a powerful mirror image of the Lincoln Memorial, enhancing its grandeur and allowing visitors to see the monument reflected in the water.

WHITE HOUSE VISITOR CENTER, WASHINGTON D.C.

The White House Visitor Center, located within the historic Baldrige Hall of the Department of Commerce building, offers a captivating window into the iconic White House in Washington D.C. This informative museum-style center provides a virtual tour and historical context for those who may not be eligible for a physical White House tour.

1450 Pennsylvania Avenue NW, Washington, DC 20004, United States - +12022081631

Closest City/Town: Washington D.C.

Best Time to Visit:

• The White House Visitor Center is open daily from 9:30 am to 4:30 pm, except for Thanksgiving Day, December 25th, and New Year's Day.

• Weekdays tend to be less crowded than weekends, especially during peak tourist season.

Getting Around:

•**Metro:** Take the Metro's Blue or Orange Line to Federal Triangle station (preferred) or Metro Center station. The Visitor Center is a short walk from either station (about 10-15 minutes).

- **Walking/Biking:** The Visitor Center is situated near the White House, making it accessible on foot or by renting a bike.

- **Car:** Parking can be limited, especially during peak season. Consider using public transportation, ride-sharing services, or biking if possible.

GPS Coordinates: 1450 Pennsylvania Ave NW, Washington, DC 20230 (38° 53′ 51″ N, 77° 00′ 32″ W)

Permit/Pass/Fees:

- Entry to the White House Visitor Center is free.

Website: For current hours, information on exhibits, and educational programs, visit the White House Historical Association website: https://www.whitehousehistory.org/

Fun Facts about the White House Visitor Center:

- Opened in 2014, the center features interactive exhibits, a large-scale model of the White House, historical artifacts, and a museum shop.

- Visitors can learn about the history of the White House, its architecture, the lives of the presidents and their families, and the traditions associated with this iconic landmark.

- The White House Visitor Center serves as a valuable resource for those interested in learning more about the presidency and the history of the United States.

FORD'S THEATRE, WASHINGTON D.C.

Ford's Theatre, situated in the heart of Washington D.C.'s vibrant Downtown district, holds a significant place in American history. More than just a theatre, it's a historic site commemorating the assassination of President Abraham Lincoln on April 14, 1865. Today, it serves as a working theatre, museum, and educational center.

511 10th St NW, Washington, DC 20004, United States - +12023474833

Closest City/Town: Washington D.C.

Best Time to Visit:

• Performances and tours are offered year-round, but schedules vary.

• Weekdays tend to be less crowded than weekends, especially during peak tourist season.

• Check the official website for current showtimes and tour availability: https://fords.org/visit-us/plan-your-visit/

Details on Getting Around:

- **Metro:** Take the Metro's Red, Blue, or Orange Line to Metro Center station. Ford's Theatre is a short walk from the station (about 5 minutes).

- **Walking/Biking:** The theatre is situated in Downtown D.C., making it easily accessible on foot or by renting a bike.

- **Car:** Street parking can be limited, especially on weekends and evenings when there are performances. Consider using public transportation, ride-sharing services, or biking if possible.

GPS Coordinates: 511 10th St NW, Washington, DC 20004 (38° 53′ 53″ N, 77° 00′ 26″ W)

Permit/Pass/Fees:

- Ticket prices vary depending on the performance or tour you choose. You can purchase tickets online in advance: https://fords.org/visit-us/plan-your-visit/

- Museum admission (when available) may have separate fees.

Website: For current hours, information on performances, tours, tickets, and the history of the site, visit the Ford's Theatre website: https://fords.org/visit-us/plan-your-visit/

Fun Facts about Ford's Theatre:

- Originally built in 1833 as a Baptist church, John T. Ford purchased it and converted it into a theater in 1859, naming it Ford's Athenaeum.

- President Lincoln was assassinated by John Wilkes Booth while watching the play "Our American Cousin" at Ford's Theatre.

- After the assassination, the theatre was used as a federal government office building for decades.

- The Ford's Theatre Society was founded in 1960 and worked towards restoring the theatre to its original appearance.

- Today, Ford's Theatre is not only a historic site but also a venue for live performances, educational programs, and special events.

WASHINGTON TRAVEL JOURNAL

Date: .... Transport: ....

| Weather |

Checklist For This Trip

Places:

Notes

Special Memories

SMITHSONIAN'S NATIONAL POSTAL MUSEUM, WASHINGTON D.C.

Delve into the captivating story of communication and postal service at the Smithsonian's National Postal Museum, situated opposite Union Station in Washington D.C. This museum houses the world's largest and most comprehensive collection of stamps and philatelic material, offering an engaging exploration of how mail has connected people throughout history.

2 Massachusetts Ave NE, Washington, DC 20002, United States - +12026335555

Closest City/Town: Washington D.C.

Best Time to Visit:

• The museum is open daily from 10:00 am to 5:30 pm, except for December 25th.

• Weekdays tend to be less crowded than weekends, especially during peak tourist season.

Getting Around:

• **Metro:** Take the Metro's Red Line to Union Station and use the Massachusetts Avenue exit – the museum is right across the street.

- **Walking/Biking:** The museum is situated next to Union Station, making it easily accessible on foot or by renting a bike.

- **Car:** Parking can be limited, especially during peak season. Consider using public transportation, ride-sharing services, or biking if possible.

GPS Coordinates: 2 Massachusetts Ave. NE, Washington, DC 20002 (38° 53′ 23″ N, 77° 00′ 24″ W)

Permit/Pass/Fees:

- Admission to the National Postal Museum is free.

- Special exhibits may require a separate ticketed admission.

Website: For current hours, information on exhibits, educational programs, and special events, visit the Smithsonian's National Postal Museum website: https://postalmuseum.si.edu/

Fun Facts about the National Postal Museum:

- Established in 1993, the museum showcases the rich history of the U.S. Postal Service and the evolution of communication technologies.

- Visitors can explore iconic artifacts like stagecoaches, mail trucks, and vintage airplanes used for mail transport.

- The museum boasts the William H. Gross Stamp Gallery, the world's largest, where visitors can learn about stamp collecting and design their own virtual stamp.

- Interactive exhibits and educational programs bring the world of mail to life for visitors of all ages.

- The National Postal Museum serves as a fascinating repository of communication history, showcasing the power of mail to connect people and societies across time and distance.

FRIENDSHIP ARCHWAY, WASHINGTON D.C.

Standing proudly as an entrance to Washington D.C.'s Chinatown neighborhood, the Friendship Archway is a vibrant landmark steeped in cultural significance. This colorful gate, constructed in 1986, serves as a symbol of friendship between Washington D.C. and its sister city, Beijing, China.

728-730 7th St NW, Washington, DC 20001, United States - +12027783150

Closest City/Town: Washington D.C. (Chinatown neighborhood)

Best Time to Visit:

- The archway is accessible 24 hours a day, year-round.

- Consider visiting during daylight hours for the best views of the ornate details and surrounding neighborhood.

- Weekdays tend to be less crowded than weekends, especially during peak tourist season.

Getting Around:

- **Metro:** Take the Metro's Red, Green, or Yellow Line to Gallery Place-Chinatown station. The archway is a short walk from the station (about 5 minutes east on H Street).

- **Walking/Biking:** The archway is situated at the eastern edge of Chinatown, making it easily accessible on foot or by renting a bike.

- **Car:** Street parking can be limited, especially during peak season. Consider using public transportation, ride-sharing services, or biking if possible.

GPS Coordinates: 7th St & H St NW, Washington, DC 20004 (38° 53′ 51″ N, 77° 00′ 22″ W)

Permit/Pass/Fees:

- There is no entrance fee to visit the Friendship Archway, as it's a publicly accessible monument.

Website:

- While there's no dedicated website for the Friendship Archway itself, you can find information about it on websites focused on D.C. tourism or Chinatown:
    - Greater Greater Washington: https://ggwash.org/
    - DCist: https://dcist.com/

Fun Facts about the Friendship Archway:

- Designed in the traditional Chinese paifang style, the archway features intricate decorations and symbolic imagery representing good fortune, longevity, and prosperity.

- The archway was constructed through a collaborative effort between the People's Republic of China and the local Chinese Consolidated Benevolent Association in D.C.

- It remains a popular spot for photos and a gateway to exploring the vibrant shops and restaurants of Washington D.C.'s Chinatown neighborhood.

- The Friendship Archway serves as a lasting symbol of cultural exchange and the strong ties between the United States and China.

HIRSHHORN MUSEUM AND SCULPTURE GARDEN, WASHINGTON D.C.

Situated beside the National Mall in Washington D.C., the Hirshhorn Museum and Sculpture Garden stands as a leading voice for contemporary art. This iconic cylindrical building, designed by architect Gordon Bunshaft, houses an impressive collection of modern and contemporary artwork, offering a stimulating experience for art enthusiasts.

Independence Ave SW &, 7th St SW, Washington, DC 20560, United States - +12026331000

Closest City/Town: Washington D.C.

Best Time to Visit:

- The museum is open Tuesday through Sunday, from 11:30 am to 5:30 pm.

- Weekdays tend to be less crowded than weekends, especially during peak tourist season.

- Consider visiting during special exhibition times to see the latest additions.

Details on Getting Around:

- **Metro:** Take the Metro's Blue or Orange Line to Smithsonian station. The museum is a short walk from the station (about 10 minutes).

- **Walking/Biking:** The museum is situated near the National Mall, making it easily accessible on foot or by renting a bike.

- **Car:** Street parking can be limited, especially during peak season. Consider using public transportation, ride-sharing services, or biking if possible.

GPS Coordinates: Independence Ave at 7th St SW, Washington, DC 20560 (38° 53′ 19″ N, 77° 00′ 12″ W)

Permit/Pass/Fees:

- Admission fees apply for both the museum and sculpture garden. You can purchase tickets online in advance: https://www.si.edu/museums/hirshhorn-museum-and-sculpture-garden

- Special exhibits may have separate fees.

Website: For current hours, information on exhibits, educational programs, and special events, visit the Hirshhorn Museum and Sculpture Garden website: https://www.si.edu/museums/hirshhorn-museum-and-sculpture-garden

Fun Facts about the Hirshhorn Museum and Sculpture Garden:

- Established in 1974, the museum was named after Joseph H. Hirshhorn, a prominent art collector who donated his extensive collection to the Smithsonian Institution.

- The Hirshhorn's collection focuses on post-World War II and contemporary art, featuring works by renowned artists like Pollock, Rothko, Giacometti, and Louise Bourgeois.

- The museum's cylindrical design offers a unique and spacious setting for showcasing large-scale installations and sculptures.

- The adjoining Sculpture Garden provides a beautiful outdoor space to explore works by modern and contemporary sculptors.

- The Hirshhorn Museum and Sculpture Garden serves as a dynamic platform for contemporary art, fostering creativity and engaging audiences with thought-provoking exhibitions and programs.

NATIONAL ARCHIVES MUSEUM, WASHINGTON D.C.

Standing north of the National Mall in Washington D.C., the National Archives Museum safeguards and showcases some of the most treasured documents of the United States. This grand building houses the Charters of Freedom, including the Declaration of Independence, the United States Constitution, and the Bill of Rights. The museum also offers a range of exhibits exploring the history and impact of these documents, and the National Archives itself holds a vast collection of historical records.

701 Constitution Ave. NW, Washington, DC 20408, United States - +12023575000

Closest City/Town: Washington D.C.

Best Time to Visit:

- The museum is open daily from 10:00 am to 5:30 pm, with limited capacity.

- Reserve timed entry tickets online in advance, especially during peak tourist season: https://museum.archives.gov/reservations-and-tours

- Weekdays tend to be less crowded than weekends.

Details on Getting Around:

- **Metro:** Take the Metro's Red Line to Judiciary Square station. The museum is a short walk from the station (about 10 minutes east).

- **Walking/Biking:** The museum is situated north of the National Mall, making it accessible on foot or by renting a bike.

- **Car:** Street parking can be limited, especially during peak season. Consider using public transportation, ride-sharing services, or biking if possible.

GPS Coordinates: 701 Constitution Ave. NW, Washington, DC 20408 (38° 53′ 42″ N, 77° 00′ 23″ W)

Permit/Pass/Fees:

- There is no entrance fee to visit the National Archives Museum itself.

- However, research room access in the National Archives building may require fees.

Website: For current hours, information on exhibits, educational programs, and special events, visit the National Archives Museum website: https://museum.archives.gov/visit

Fun Facts about the National Archives Museum:

- Established in 1938, the National Archives Museum serves as the public face of the National Archives and Records Administration.

- The Charters of Freedom Rotunda is a highlight, showcasing the original Declaration of Independence, Constitution, and Bill of Rights under carefully controlled conditions.

- The museum also features rotating exhibits exploring various aspects of U.S. history and government through original documents, photographs, and artifacts.

- The vast holdings of the National Archives itself include records from all three branches of the federal government, dating back to the nation's founding.

- The National Archives Museum serves as a powerful reminder of the importance of preserving historical documents and the enduring legacy of the United States' founding principles.

JOHN F. KENNEDY CENTER FOR THE PERFORMING ARTS, WASHINGTON D.C.

Standing majestically on the banks of the Potomac River in Washington D.C., the John F. Kennedy Center for the Performing Arts serves as the national cultural center of the United States. This iconic complex honors President John F. Kennedy's vision for a national space dedicated to the performing arts. Across its multiple theaters, the Kennedy Center stages a wide variety of performances, from theater and dance to music, opera, and ballet.

2700 F St NW, Washington, DC 20566, United States - +12024674600

Closest City/Town: Washington D.C.

Best Time to Visit:

- The Kennedy Center offers performances throughout the year, so the best time to visit depends on the specific show you'd like to see.

- Check the official performance calendar to plan your visit: https://www.kennedy-center.org/

- Weekday performances tend to be less crowded than weekends, especially during peak tourist season.

Details on Getting Around:

- **Metro:** Take the Metro's Blue or Orange Line to Foggy Bottom station. The Kennedy Center is a short walk from the station (about 5 minutes). A free shuttle bus service is also available from the Foggy Bottom Metro stop.

- **Walking/Biking:** The Kennedy Center is situated along the Potomac River, making it accessible on foot or by renting a bike.

- **Car:** Parking can be limited, especially for evening performances. Consider using public transportation, ride-sharing services, or biking if possible.

GPS Coordinates: 2700 F St NW, Washington, DC 20566 (38° 53′ 27″ N, 77° 03′ 32″ W)

Permit/Pass/Fees:

- Ticket prices vary depending on the performance you choose. You can purchase tickets online in advance: https://www.kennedy-center.org/

Website: For current hours, information on performances, tickets, and the Kennedy Center's history, visit the official website: https://www.kennedy-center.org/

Fun Facts about the John F. Kennedy Center for the Performing Arts:

- Opened in 1971, the Kennedy Center boasts multiple theaters, including the Opera House, Concert Hall, Eisenhower Theater, and Terrace Theater, offering a diverse range of performance spaces.

- Besides renowned performances, the Kennedy Center offers educational programs, lectures, and workshops throughout the year.

- The building itself is a landmark of modern architecture, designed by architect Edward Durell Stone.

- The Kennedy Center serves as a national stage, showcasing the best of American and international performing arts, and fostering artistic expression and cultural exchange.

WASHINGTON TRAVEL JOURNAL

Date: .... Transport: ....

Weather

Checklist For This Trip

Places:

Notes

Special Memories

NATIONAL GALLERY OF ART – SCULPTURE GARDEN, WASHINGTON D.C.

Situated on the National Mall between the West Building of the National Gallery of Art and the Smithsonian Institution's National Museum of Natural History, the National Gallery of Art – Sculpture Garden offers a unique blend of art and nature. This 6.1-acre outdoor space showcases a collection of large-scale modern and contemporary sculptures, creating a dynamic and visually striking experience.

Constitution Ave NW &, 7th St NW, Washington, DC 20408, United States - +12022893360

Closest City/Town: Washington D.C.

Best Time to Visit:

• The Sculpture Garden is open daily from sunrise to sunset, year-round, making it a great option for any time of day.

• Consider visiting during pleasant weather conditions to fully enjoy the outdoor setting.

• Weekdays tend to be less crowded than weekends, especially during peak tourist season.

Details on Getting Around:

- **Metro:** Take the Metro's Blue, Orange, or Silver Line to Metro Center station. From there, it's a short walk or ride-sharing service trip to the Sculpture Garden (about 10-15 minutes).

- **Walking/Biking:** The Sculpture Garden is situated near the National Mall, making it easily accessible on foot or by renting a bike.

- **Car:** Parking can be limited near the National Mall, especially during peak season. Consider using public transportation, ride-sharing services, or biking if possible.

GPS Coordinates: 700 Constitution Ave NW, Washington, DC 20560 (38° 53′ 27″ N, 77° 00′ 11″ W)

Permit/Pass/Fees:

- There is no entrance fee to visit the National Gallery of Art – Sculpture Garden. It's free and open to the public.

Website: For information about the Sculpture Garden's collection, special events, and the National Gallery of Art, visit the National Gallery of Art website: https://www.nga.gov/visit/tours-and-guides/national-gallery-sculpture-garden.html

Fun Facts about the National Gallery of Art – Sculpture Garden:

- Completed and opened to the public in 1999, the Sculpture Garden was designed by landscape architect Laurie Olin to complement the existing National Gallery buildings.

- The collection features works by renowned sculptors like Alexander Calder, Louise Bourgeois, Tony Smith, and Roy Lichtenstein.

- A central reflecting pool (which serves as an ice-skating rink in the winter) adds another visual element to the garden's design.

- The Sculpture Garden offers a unique opportunity to experience art in a public, open-air setting, fostering appreciation for modern and contemporary sculpture.

- With its blend of art, nature, and accessibility, the National Gallery of Art – Sculpture Garden is a popular destination for locals and tourists alike.

WATERMELON HOUSE, WASHINGTON D.C.

Located in the Logan Circle neighborhood of Washington D.C., the Watermelon House is a charming row house adorned with a larger-than-life mural of a watermelon. This vibrant landmark has become a popular social media hotspot and a delightful surprise for strollers in the area.

1112 Q St NW, Washington, DC 20009, United States - +12026561256

Closest City/Town: Washington D.C. (Logan Circle neighborhood)

Best Time to Visit:

• The house itself is a private residence, but you can admire the mural any time of day.

• Consider visiting during daylight hours for the best photo opportunities with the colorful mural.

• Weekends tend to be busier than weekdays, especially with people taking photos.

Details on Getting Around:

- **Metro:** Take the Metro's Green or Yellow Line to Shaw-Howard Place station. From there, it's a short walk east on Q Street to the Watermelon House (about 5 minutes).

- **Walking/Biking:** The house is situated in Logan Circle, making it easily accessible on foot or by renting a bike.

- **Car:** Street parking can be limited, especially on weekends. Consider using public transportation, ride-sharing services, or biking if possible.

GPS Coordinates: 1112 Q St NW, Washington, DC 20009 (38° 54′ 12″ N, 77° 02′ 22″ W)

Permit/Pass/Fees:

- There is no entrance fee or permit required to view the Watermelon House from the street. It's a public art installation.

Website:

- While the Watermelon House itself doesn't have a website, you can find photos and information about it on social media and travel blogs. Consider searching for "#WatermelonHouseDC" to see what others have posted.

Fun Facts about the Watermelon House:

- The Watermelon House wasn't intended to be a public art piece. The owners originally just wanted a brighter paint color for their home. Due to a color mismatch, the pink sidewall became the base for a watermelon mural.

- The house has become a popular symbol of summer fun and creativity in the Logan Circle neighborhood.

- Many visitors participate in the #WatermelonJumps social media trend, where they take photos jumping in front of the mural.

- The Watermelon House serves as a reminder that art can be found in unexpected places and bring joy to everyday life.

OLD STONE HOUSE, WASHINGTON D.C.

Standing proudly in Georgetown, Washington D.C., the Old Stone House holds the distinction of being the oldest unchanged building structure in the nation's capital. This historic landmark, constructed in the mid-18th century, offers a glimpse into the early days of Georgetown and serves as a reminder of the city's colonial past.

3051 M St NW, Washington, DC 20007, United States - +12024266851

Closest City/Town: Washington D.C. (Georgetown neighborhood)

Best Time to Visit:

- The exterior grounds are open daily from sunrise to sunset, year-round.

- The front room, which functions as a park store, is typically open during daylight hours.

- Weekends tend to be busier than weekdays, especially during peak tourist season.

Getting Around:

- **Metro:** Take the Metro's Blue or Orange Line to Foggy Bottom station. From there, it's a moderate walk (about 20 minutes) or a short ride-sharing service trip to the Old Stone House.

- **Walking/Biking:** The Old Stone House is situated in Georgetown, a walkable neighborhood. You can also rent a bike for easier exploration.

- **Car:** Street parking can be limited, especially on weekends and during peak tourist season. Consider using public transportation, ride-sharing services, or biking if possible.

GPS Coordinates: 3051 M St NW, Washington, DC 20007 (38° 53′ 09″ N, 77° 04′ 26″ W)

Permit/Pass/Fees:

- There is no entrance fee to visit the exterior grounds of the Old Stone House.

- Purchases from the park store may incur a standard sales tax.

Website:

- For information on the Old Stone House, opening hours (which may vary), and other National Park Service sites in the area, visit the National Park Service website: https://www.nps.gov/rocr/planyourvisit/old-stone-house-visitor-center.htm?ref=travellens.co

Fun Facts about the Old Stone House:

- Built around 1765, the Old Stone House predates the official founding of Washington D.C. by nearly 30 years.

- Originally a private residence, the house has served various purposes throughout history, including a tavern and a store.

- Contrary to a popular misconception, there's no evidence to suggest George Washington ever slept at the Old Stone House.

- The building's thick stone walls, constructed from local materials, offer a testament to 18th-century construction techniques.

- The Old Stone House serves as a valuable link to Washington D.C.'s colonial past, offering a tangible connection to the city's early development.

EASTERN MARKET, WASHINGTON D.C.

Situated in the heart of Washington D.C.'s historic Capitol Hill neighborhood, Eastern Market is a vibrant marketplace boasting over 100 vendors. This bustling community hub offers a delightful mix of fresh produce, local crafts, prepared foods, and specialty shops, making it a great place to experience the sights, sounds, and flavors of D.C.

225 7th St SE, Washington, DC 20003, United States - +12026985253

Closest City/Town: Washington D.C. (Capitol Hill neighborhood)

Best Time to Visit:

- Weekends are the prime time to visit Eastern Market, when all vendors are open (including outdoor vendors) from 6:30 am to 4:00 pm.

- Weekdays offer a calmer atmosphere, with some vendors open year-round. Check the website for specific days and hours.

- Consider visiting during seasonal events like "Art All Night" or "The Holly Days" for a festive market experience.

Details on Getting Around:

- **Metro:** Take the Metro's Blue or Orange Line to Eastern Market station, which provides direct access to the market.

- **Walking/Biking:** The market is situated in Capitol Hill, making it easily accessible on foot or by renting a bike.

- **Car:** Street parking can be limited, especially on weekends. Consider using public transportation, ride-sharing services, or biking if possible.

GPS Coordinates: 225 7th St SE, Washington, DC 20003 (38° 53′ 24″ N, 77° 00′ 18″ W)

Permit/Pass/Fees:

- There is no entrance fee to visit Eastern Market itself. Individual vendors may have varying pricing for their products.

Website: For current hours, information on vendors, events, and directions, visit the Eastern Market website: https://easternmarket-dc.org/

Fun Facts about Eastern Market:

- Established in 1873, Eastern Market is one of the oldest continuously operating public markets in D.C., and the only one that retains its original function.

- The market played a significant role in feeding the city during its early years and continues to be a vital source of fresh produce for the surrounding community.

- Eastern Market is not just a marketplace, but also a social hub where residents and visitors can gather, connect, and enjoy the local culture.

- The historic market building, constructed in a 19th-century Italianate architectural style, adds to the overall charm of the Eastern Market experience.

- From fresh, local ingredients to handcrafted souvenirs, Eastern Market offers a delightful taste of what Washington D.C. has to offer.

CONSTITUTION GARDENS, WASHINGTON D.C.

Constitution Gardens, situated between the Vietnam Veterans Memorial and the World War II Memorial on the National Mall in Washington D.C., offers a peaceful escape amidst the bustling capital city. This 50-acre park, established in 1965, serves as a living legacy to the U.S. Constitution and a delightful spot for relaxation, reflection, and scenic strolls.

Constitution Ave. NW, Washington, DC 20024, United States - +12024266841

Closest City/Town: Washington D.C.

Best Time to Visit:

- Constitution Gardens is open year-round, offering a haven for visitors during any season.

- Spring and fall provide comfortable temperatures for enjoying the outdoors.

- Weekdays tend to be less crowded than weekends, especially during peak tourist season.

Getting Around:

- **Metro:** Take the Metro's Blue or Orange Line to Metro Center station. From there, it's a short walk (about 10 minutes) to Constitution Gardens.

- **Walking/Biking:** The park is situated on the National Mall, making it easily accessible on foot or by renting a bike.

- **Car:** Street parking can be limited, especially near the National Mall during peak season. Consider using public transportation, ride-sharing services, or biking if possible.

GPS Coordinates: 2 Constitution Ave NW, Washington, DC 20002 (38° 53′ 49″ N, 77° 00′ 28″ W)

Permit/Pass/Fees:

- There is no entrance fee to visit Constitution Gardens itself.

Website:

- For information on the National Mall and surrounding memorials, visit the National Park Service website: https://www.nps.gov/nama/

Fun Facts about Constitution Gardens:

- Originally, the land where Constitution Gardens now stands was part of the Potomac River. In the early 20th century, the U.S. Army Corps of Engineers dredged the area, creating space for development.

- The park's centerpiece is a reflecting pool with a central island dedicated to the 56 signers of the Declaration of Independence. Each state is represented by a stone engraved with the name of a signer from that state.

- Constitution Gardens is a popular spot for seasonal flower displays, adding a touch of color and vibrancy to the park.

- The Lockkeeper's House, located at the edge of the gardens, is the oldest building on the National Mall, dating back to the 1830s.

- Constitution Gardens offers a serene escape in the heart of Washington D.C., a place to appreciate the beauty of nature and reflect on the nation's history.

NATIONAL CAPITOL COLUMNS, WASHINGTON D.C.

Standing tall amidst the 20-acre Ellipse Meadow in Washington D.C. are the National Capitol Columns. These 22 Corinthian columns were originally part of the U.S. Capitol's East Portico, serving as a grand entrance from 1828 until 1958. Today, they offer a unique landmark and a connection to the architectural heritage of the nation's capitol building.

3501, 3501 New York Ave NE, Washington, DC 20002, United States - +12022452726

Closest City/Town: Washington D.C.

Best Time to Visit:

- The National Capitol Columns are accessible year-round, offering a scenic spot any time of day.

- Consider visiting during daylight hours for the best views of the columns and surrounding meadow.

- Weekends tend to be busier than weekdays, especially during peak tourist season.

Getting Around:

- **Metro:** Take the Metro's Red Line to Judiciary Square station. From there, it's a moderate walk (about 15-20 minutes) or a short ride-sharing service trip to the Ellipse Meadow and the National Capitol Columns.

- **Walking/Biking:** The columns are situated on the southern end of the Ellipse Meadow, making them easily accessible on foot or by renting a bike.

- **Car:** Parking can be limited near the National Mall, especially during peak season. Consider using public transportation, ride-sharing services, or biking if possible.

GPS Coordinates: 200 E Basin Dr SW, Washington, DC 20024 (38° 53′ 22″ N, 77° 00′ 23″ W)

Permit/Pass/Fees:

- There is no entrance fee to visit the National Capitol Columns, as they are part of a public park.

Website:

- For information on the National Capitol Columns and the surrounding area, you can visit the U.S. National Arboretum website or general Washington D.C. tourism websites:

  - U.S. National Arboretum: https://www.ars.usda.gov/northeast-area/washington-dc/national-arboretum/

  - General DC Information: https://washington.org/

Fun Facts about the National Capitol Columns:

- Quarried from sandstone near Aquia Creek in Virginia, the columns were transported to Washington D.C. by barge in the early days of the nation's capital.

- The original construction of the East Portico with these columns was overseen by famous architect Charles Bulfinch, who also designed the Maine State House.

- When the U.S. Capitol dome was completed in 1866, it appeared inadequately supported by the existing columns. This led to the East Portico's expansion in 1958, and the removal of the original columns to their current location on the Ellipse Meadow.

- The National Capitol Columns stand as a testament to the architectural evolution of the U.S. Capitol and a reminder of the ongoing preservation efforts for our nation's historic buildings.

- Offering a picturesque backdrop for photos and a tranquil spot for reflection, the National Capitol Columns add a unique touch to Washington D.C.'s green spaces.

WASHINGTON TRAVEL JOURNAL

Date:.................................... Transport:....................................

Weather

Checklist For This Trip

Places:

Notes

Special Memories

HEURICH HOUSE MUSEUM, WASHINGTON D.C.

Standing proudly in the Dupont Circle neighborhood of Washington D.C., the Heurich House Museum, also known as the Christian Heurich Mansion or Brewmaster's Castle, is a captivating landmark steeped in history. This grand Victorian mansion, built between 1892 and 1894, served as the home of Christian Heurich, a successful German immigrant brewer who became a prominent figure in D.C.'s social and industrial scene. Today, the Heurich House Museum offers a glimpse into the opulent lifestyle of the Gilded Age and the fascinating story of the Heurich family.

1307 New Hampshire Ave NW, Washington, DC 20036, United States - +12024291894

Closest City/Town: Washington D.C. (Dupont Circle neighborhood)

Best Time to Visit:

- The museum is open Thursdays, Fridays, and Saturdays from 11:00 am to 3:00 pm.

- Consider visiting during these hours to ensure access to the mansion tours.

- Weekdays tend to be less crowded than weekends, especially during peak tourist season.

Details on Getting Around:

- **Metro:** Take the Metro's Red Line to Dupont Circle South station. The museum is a short walk from the station (about 5 minutes east on H Street).

- **Walking/Biking:** The Heurich House is situated in Dupont Circle, making it easily accessible on foot or by renting a bike.

- **Car:** Street parking can be limited, especially during peak season. Consider using public transportation, ride-sharing services, or biking if possible.

GPS Coordinates: 1307 New Hampshire Ave. NW, Washington, DC 20036 (38° 53' 51" N, 77° 00' 22" W)

Permit/Pass/Fees:

- Admission fees apply for tours of the Heurich House Museum. You can purchase tickets online in advance: https://heurichhouse.org/

Website:

- For current hours, information on tours, exhibits, and educational programs, visit the Heurich House Museum website: https://heurichhouse.org/

Fun Facts about the Heurich House Museum:

- Designed by architect John Granville Meyers in the Richardsonian Romanesque style, the Heurich House is one of the most intact Victorian mansions in the country.

- The mansion boasts opulent interiors featuring intricate woodwork, stained glass windows, and decorative tilework, reflecting the Heurich family's wealth and social status.

- Christian Heurich was not only a successful brewer but also a philanthropist who played a significant role in the development of D.C.

- The Heurich House Museum offers a unique opportunity to step back in time and experience the grandeur of the Gilded Age in Washington D.C.

- Beyond the mansion tours, the museum also hosts special events and educational programs that delve deeper into the history of brewing, the Heurich family, and the Gilded Age era.

KENILWORTH PARK & AQUATIC GARDENS, WASHINGTON D.C.

Situated along the eastern bank of the Anacostia River in Washington D.C., Kenilworth Park & Aquatic Gardens offers a peaceful escape amidst the urban landscape. This 700-acre park encompasses vibrant aquatic plant life, tidal marshes, recreational facilities, and a rich history. Kenilworth Park is a haven for nature enthusiasts, offering a chance to spot wildlife, explore serene gardens, and learn about the importance of wetlands.

1550 Anacostia Ave NE, Washington, DC 20019, United States - +12026926080

Closest City/Town: Washington D.C. (Northeastern corner, near Maryland border)

Best Time to Visit:

- Kenilworth Park & Aquatic Gardens is open year-round, except for January 1, Thanksgiving, and December 25.

- Spring and summer offer the opportunity to see the lotus flowers in bloom (typically late June to July).

- Fall provides crisp air and vibrant foliage, while winter allows for peaceful birdwatching.

- Weekdays tend to be less crowded than weekends, especially during peak tourist season.

Getting Around:

- **Metro:** Take the Metro's Green Line to Greenbelt station. From there, it's a bus ride or ride-sharing service trip to the park entrance (about a 15-20 minute commute).

- **Car:** Parking is available at the park, but it can fill up on busy days. Consider using public transportation or ride-sharing services if possible.

GPS Coordinates: 400 Anacostia Ave NE, Washington, DC 20002 (38° 53′ 42″ N, 76° 56′ 23″ W)

Permit/Pass/Fees:

- There is no entrance fee to visit Kenilworth Park & Aquatic Gardens itself.

Website:

- For current hours, information on the gardens, trails, events, and accessibility, visit the National Park Service website: https://www.nps.gov/keaq/

Fun Facts about Kenilworth Park & Aquatic Gardens:

- The park's origins date back to the L'Enfant Plan for Washington D.C. in 1791. The Aquatic Gardens were originally a commercial water garden before being acquired by the National Park Service in 1938.

- Kenilworth Park boasts the only National Park Service site dedicated solely to the cultivation and display of aquatic plants.

- The park features over 45 ponds showcasing a diverse collection of water lilies and lotus flowers.

- Kenilworth Marsh, the largest remaining tidal marsh in D.C., is a valuable natural habitat for birds, fish, and other wildlife.

- Kenilworth Park & Aquatic Gardens serves as an urban oasis, promoting environmental education, appreciation for wetland ecosystems, and opportunities for peaceful recreation.

THE MOONGATE GARDEN, WASHINGTON D.C.

Tucked within the Enid A. Haupt Garden, located between the Smithsonian Castle and the Freer|Sackler Gallery on the National Mall in Washington D.C., lies the Moongate Garden. This serene hidden gem draws inspiration from Chinese garden design, offering a place for peaceful contemplation and a unique cultural experience.

1200 Jefferson Dr SW, Washington, DC 20024, United States - +12026332220

Closest City/Town: Washington D.C.

Best Time to Visit:

• The Moongate Garden is accessible during the same hours as the Enid A. Haupt Garden, typically from 10:00 am to 5:00 pm daily.

• Consider visiting on a clear day to fully appreciate the reflection of the sky and, of course, the moon, in the central pool.

• Weekdays tend to be less crowded than weekends, especially during peak tourist season.

Getting Around:

- **Metro:** Take the Metro's Yellow or Blue Line to Smithsonian station. From there, it's a short walk (about 10 minutes south) to the Enid A. Haupt Garden and the Moongate Garden.

- **Walking/Biking:** The Moongate Garden is situated on the National Mall, making it easily accessible on foot or by renting a bike.

- **Car:** Street parking can be limited, especially near the National Mall during peak season. Consider using public transportation, ride-sharing services, or biking if possible.

GPS Coordinates: Enid A. Haupt Garden: 750 Independence Ave SW, Washington, DC 20560 (38° 53′ 19″ N, 77° 00′ 27″ W)

Permit/Pass/Fees:

- There is no entrance fee to visit the Moongate Garden itself, as it's part of the Enid A. Haupt Garden.

Website:

- For information on the Enid A. Haupt Garden hours, events, and accessibility, visit the Smithsonian Gardens website: https://www.si.edu/museums/smithsonian-gardens

Fun Facts about The Moongate Garden:

- Inspired by the Temple of Heaven in Beijing, China, the Moongate Garden features circular structures ("moongates") and a central pool that reflects the sky and moonlit evenings.

- The use of granite and water in the garden design reflects traditional Chinese symbolism of these elements representing the earth and spirit, respectively.

- The Moongate Garden offers a unique blend of tranquility and cultural significance within the bustling National Mall environment.

- While small in size, the Moongate Garden provides a delightful escape for visitors seeking a moment of peace and a glimpse of Chinese garden aesthetics.

- Pay attention to the placement of the moongates, as they are strategically positioned to frame important features of the surrounding landscape.

BASILICA OF THE NATIONAL SHRINE OF THE IMMACULATE CONCEPTION, WASHINGTON D.C.

Standing majestically on the grounds of the Catholic University of America in Washington D.C., the Basilica of the National Shrine of the Immaculate Conception is a landmark of faith, history, and architectural wonder. This colossal Roman Catholic church, the largest Catholic house of worship in North America, serves as a national sanctuary and a place of pilgrimage for people of all faiths.

400 Michigan Ave NE, Washington, DC 20017, United States - +12025268300

Closest City/Town: Washington D.C. (Brookland neighborhood)

Best Time to Visit:

• The Basilica is open 365 days a year, offering daily Masses and extended visiting hours.

• Weekdays tend to be less crowded than weekends, especially during peak tourist season.

• Consider attending a Mass to experience the spiritual atmosphere (schedules available online).

• Guided tours are offered and provide insightful information about the Basilica's history and architecture.

Details on Getting Around:

- **Metro:** Take the Metro's Red Line to Brookland-CUA station. The Basilica is a short walk (about 10 minutes north) from the station.

- **Bus:** Several Metrobus lines stop near the Basilica.

- **Car:** Limited street parking is available in the surrounding area. Consider using public transportation or ride-sharing services if possible.

GPS Coordinates: 400 Michigan Ave NE, Washington, DC 20017 (38° 54′ 08″ N, 77° 00′ 07″ W)

Permit/Pass/Fees:

- There is no entrance fee to visit the Basilica itself. Donations are gratefully accepted.

Website:

- For information on Mass times, guided tours, events, and the Basilica's history, visit the official website: https://www.nationalshrine.org/

Fun Facts about the Basilica of the National Shrine of the Immaculate Conception:

- Construction began in 1920 and spanned over 70 years, with influences from Byzantine and Romanesque architectural styles.

- The Basilica boasts stained glass windows depicting stories from the Bible and American Catholic history.

- A 56-bell carillon offers melodic chimes throughout the day.

- The Crypt Church, located beneath the Basilica, offers a unique sacred space with its own distinct architecture and artwork.

- As a national shrine, the Basilica has welcomed Popes, presidents, and countless pilgrims, serving as a symbol of faith and unity.

THE KREEGER MUSEUM, WASHINGTON D.C.

The Kreeger Museum is a non-profit haven for modern and contemporary art, Situated in the Foxhall Road neighborhood of Washington D.C. Housed in a stunning mid-century mansion designed by renowned architect Philip Johnson, the museum offers a unique blend of art, history, and architecture.

WWC6+QF Washington, District of Columbia, USA - +12023373050

Founded in 1994, the Kreeger Museum showcases the extensive art collection of David and Carmen Lloyd Kreeger, prominent figures in D.C.'s cultural scene. Their collection features works from the 19th and 20th centuries, with a focus on European and American paintings, sculptures, and decorative arts.

Highlights of the Kreeger Collection:

- Paintings by Claude Monet, Vincent van Gogh, Pablo Picasso, and Edgar Degas
- Sculptures by Auguste Rodin, Alexander Calder, and Alberto Giacometti
- Works by prominent American artists like Mary Cassatt and Childe Hassam

Beyond the permanent collection, the Kreeger Museum also hosts:

- Temporary exhibitions featuring a variety of modern and contemporary artists.
- Educational programs and lectures for visitors of all ages.
- Special events and concerts throughout the year.

Here's some helpful information for planning your visit:

- **Website:** https://www.kreegermuseum.org/
- **Location:** 38° 54′ 12″ N, 77° 02′ 22″ W (1112 Q St NW, Washington, DC 20009)
- **Closest Metro:** Take the Metro's Green or Yellow Line to Shaw-Howard Place station (about a 5-minute walk to the museum).
- **Hours:** Open Wednesday through Sunday, from 11:00 am to 5:00 pm. Closed Mondays and Tuesdays.
- **Admission Fee:** There is a general admission fee, with discounts for seniors, students, and groups. Free admission is offered on the first Thursday of every month.

Interesting Facts about the Kreeger Museum:

- The building that houses the museum was originally designed as a private residence for the Kreeger family.
- The mansion's design incorporates elements of the International Style, characterized by clean lines, open spaces, and an emphasis on natural light.
- The Kreeger Museum's sculpture garden offers a delightful outdoor space to enjoy art amidst a serene setting.
- The museum has been featured in several films and television shows, including "The Exorcist" and "House of Cards."

Whether you're a seasoned art enthusiast or simply curious to explore a unique cultural gem, the Kreeger Museum offers a rewarding experience for visitors of all backgrounds.

THE NATIONAL CHRISTMAS TREE, WASHINGTON D.C.

Standing tall on the Ellipse near the White House in Washington D.C. is the National Christmas Tree, a beloved tradition that brings festive cheer to the nation's capital every December. This tradition dates back to 1923, when President Calvin Coolidge first lit a Christmas tree on the Ellipse to spread holiday spirit during a challenging time.

15th St NW &, E St NW, Washington, DC 20500, United States - +12027962500

Closest City/Town: Washington D.C.

Best Time to Visit:

- The National Christmas Tree and surrounding trees are illuminated nightly from early December until early January. The exact dates can vary slightly from year to year.

- Consider visiting during the lighting ceremony, typically held in early December, for a festive experience.

- Weekdays tend to be less crowded than weekends, especially closer to Christmas.

Details on Getting Around:

- **Metro:** Take the Metro's Blue or Orange Line to Metro Center station. From there, it's a moderate walk (about 15-20 minutes) or a short ride-sharing service trip to the Ellipse and the National Christmas Tree.

- **Walking/Biking:** The Ellipse is situated near the White House, making it easily accessible on foot or by renting a bike.

- **Car:** Street parking can be limited, especially near the National Mall during peak season. Consider using public transportation, ride-sharing services, or biking if possible.

GPS Coordinates: 38° 53' 52" N, 77° 00' 27" W (Ellipse at 15th St NW, Washington, DC 20500)

Permit/Pass/Fees:

- There is no entrance fee to visit the National Christmas Tree and the Ellipse.

Website:

- For information on the lighting ceremony, tree illumination schedule, and holiday events, visit the Pageant of Peace website: https://www.thenationaltree.org/

Fun Facts about the National Christmas Tree:

- The National Christmas Tree is typically a spruce tree, though the specific species may vary.

- Each year, one-of-a-kind ornaments representing every U.S. state, territory, and the District of Columbia are created and displayed on the tree.

- The National Christmas Tree lighting ceremony is a televised event that features musical performances and remarks by dignitaries.

- The tradition of the National Christmas Tree serves as a symbol of unity and hope during the holiday season.

- In addition to the main tree, the Ellipse is adorned with dozens of smaller trees representing various states and organizations, adding to the festive atmosphere.

GEORGETOWN WATERFRONT PARK, WASHINGTON D.C.

Georgetown Waterfront Park, a 10-acre national park Situated along the banks of the Potomac River in Washington D.C., offers a charming escape in the heart of the historic Georgetown neighborhood. This scenic park, completed in 2011, provides a place for relaxation, recreation, and stunning waterfront views.

3303 Water St NW, Washington, DC 20007, United States - +12028956000

Closest City/Town: Washington D.C. (Georgetown neighborhood)

Best Time to Visit:

- Georgetown Waterfront Park is a year-round destination, offering something for every season.

- Spring and fall provide comfortable temperatures for enjoying outdoor activities.

- Weekends are lively with vendors and events, while weekdays offer a calmer atmosphere.

- Summer brings the park's iconic fountain to life, perfect for a refreshing splash on hot days.

Details on Getting Around:

- **Metro:** Take the Metro's Blue or Orange Line to Georgetown Waterfront station, providing direct access to the park.

- **Walking/Biking:** The park's location within Georgetown makes it easily accessible on foot or by renting a bike.

- **Car:** Street parking can be limited, especially on weekends. Consider using public transportation, ride-sharing services, or biking if possible.

GPS Coordinates: 38° 53′ 24″ N, 77° 00′ 18″ W (Wisconsin Ave NW & K St NW, Washington, DC 20007)

Permit/Pass/Fees:

- There is no entrance fee to visit Georgetown Waterfront Park itself. Individual vendors may have varying pricing for their products or rentals.

Website:

- For information on park events, hours, and accessibility, visit the National Park Service website: https://www.nps.gov/gwmp/

Fun Facts about Georgetown Waterfront Park:

- The park's design incorporates sustainable features like rain gardens to manage stormwater runoff.

- A centerpiece of the park is the interactive fountain, a popular spot for children and adults alike to cool off during the summer.

- The Key Bridge Boathouse, located at the park's western edge, offers kayak, canoe, and paddleboard rentals, allowing visitors to explore the Potomac River from a different perspective.

- Georgetown Waterfront Park serves as a venue for various events throughout the year, including art shows, concerts, and seasonal celebrations.

- From leisurely strolls and picnics to kayaking and enjoying live music, Georgetown Waterfront Park offers a delightful mix of relaxation and recreation along the scenic Potomac River.

WASHINGTON TRAVEL JOURNAL

Date: .... Transport: ....

Weather					

Checklist For This Trip

Places:

Notes

Special Memories

AFRICAN AMERICAN CIVIL WAR MUSEUM, WASHINGTON D.C.

The African American Civil War Museum, also known as the African American Civil War Memorial Museum (AACWM), stands proudly in the U Street neighborhood of Washington D.C. This museum serves as a crucial repository of history, honoring the significant contributions of African American soldiers, sailors, and civilians during the Civil War.

1925 Vermont Ave NW, Washington, DC 20001, United States - +12026672667

Closest City/Town: Washington D.C. (U Street neighborhood)

Best Time to Visit:

• The museum is open Wednesday through Sunday, from 10:00 am to 4:00 pm.

• Consider visiting during these hours to ensure access to exhibits and programs.

• Weekdays tend to be less crowded than weekends, especially during peak tourist season.

Getting Around:

- **Metro:** Take the Metro's Green or Yellow Line to U Street/African American Civil War Memorial station. The museum is located right next to the station.

- **Walking/Biking:** The museum is situated in the U Street corridor, making it easily accessible on foot or by renting a bike.

- **Car:** Street parking can be limited, especially during peak season. Consider using public transportation, ride-sharing services, or biking if possible.

GPS Coordinates: 1925 Vermont Ave NW, Washington, DC 20001 (38° 54′ 59″ N, 77° 01′ 33″ W)

Permit/Pass/Fees:

- Admission fees apply for entrance to the African American Civil War Museum. You can purchase tickets online in advance or at the museum entrance: https://afroamcivilwar.org/

Website:

- For current hours, information on exhibits, educational programs, and the museum's mission, visit the African American Civil War Memorial Museum website: https://afroamcivilwar.org/

Fun Facts about the African American Civil War Museum:

- Established in 1999, the museum aims to rectify the historical oversight of excluding the vital role of African Americans in the Civil War.

- The museum's centerpiece is a memorial wall inscribed with the names of over 209,000 African American soldiers and sailors who fought for the Union.

- Exhibits explore the experiences of African Americans before, during, and after the Civil War, highlighting their struggles for freedom and equality.

- The museum offers educational programs and events throughout the year, fostering a deeper understanding of this critical period in American history.

- The African American Civil War Museum stands as a testament to the bravery, sacrifice, and resilience of African Americans who helped shape the nation's destiny.

UNITED STATES NAVY MEMORIAL PLAZA, WASHINGTON D.C.

Standing proudly on Pennsylvania Avenue NW, midway between the White House and the Capitol Building, is the United States Navy Memorial Plaza. This commemorative space honors the men and women who have served or are currently serving in the Navy, Marine Corps, Coast Guard, and the Merchant Marine.

701 Pennsylvania Avenue NW, Washington, DC 20004, United States - +12027372300

Closest City/Town: Washington D.C.

Best Time to Visit:

- The Navy Memorial Plaza is accessible year-round, offering a scenic spot any time of day.

- Consider visiting during daylight hours for the best views of the plaza, surrounding architecture, and potential events.

- Weekends tend to be busier than weekdays, especially during peak tourist season.

Getting Around:

- **Metro:** Take the Metro's Red Line to Archives station. The plaza is a short walk (about 5 minutes south) from the station.

- **Walking/Biking:** The Navy Memorial Plaza is situated on Pennsylvania Avenue, making it easily accessible on foot or by renting a bike.

- **Car:** Parking can be limited near the National Mall, especially during peak season. Consider using public transportation, ride-sharing services, or biking if possible.

GPS Coordinates: 701 Pennsylvania Ave NW, Washington, DC 20004 (38° 53′ 39″ N, 77° 01′ 23″ W)

Permit/Pass/Fees:

- There is no entrance fee to visit the Navy Memorial Plaza itself.

Website:

- For information on the Navy Memorial Plaza, the surrounding memorial structures, and the Navy Memorial's mission, visit their website: https://www.navymemorial.org/

Fun Facts about the US Navy Memorial Plaza:

- The plaza features a granite map of the world, depicting the oceans as a reminder of the Navy's global reach.

- A central plaza serves as a stage for wreath-laying ceremonies, Navy Band concerts, and outdoor movie screenings, all with the backdrop of the National Archives Building.

- Overlooking the plaza is the original Lone Sailor statue, a stirring tribute to all personnel of the sea services.

- The surrounding area features fountains honoring the U.S. Navy and the navies of the world, along with bronze high reliefs commemorating various events, personnel, and communities of the sea services.

- The Navy Memorial Plaza serves as a popular gathering space for veterans, their families, and visitors seeking to learn more about the rich history and ongoing legacy of America's sea services.

WASHINGTON MONUMENT GROUNDS, WASHINGTON D.C.

Standing tall amidst 106 acres of parkland, the Washington Monument Grounds is a cultural landscape within the National Mall in Washington D.C. This historic district serves as a beautiful green space and a significant landmark honoring the nation's first president, George Washington.

130 17th St NW, Washington, DC 20006, United States - +12024266841

Closest City/Town: Washington D.C.

Best Time to Visit:

- The Washington Monument Grounds are open year-round, offering a scenic escape any time of day.

- Consider visiting during daylight hours for the best views of the monument and the surrounding grounds.

- Spring offers blossoming cherry trees, while fall brings vibrant foliage. Weekends tend to be busier than weekdays, especially during peak tourist season.

Details on Getting Around:

- **Metro:** Take the Metro's Blue or Orange Line to Smithsonian station. From there, it's a short walk (about 10 minutes south) to the Washington Monument Grounds.

- **Walking/Biking:** The monument grounds are situated on the National Mall, making them easily accessible on foot or by renting a bike.

- **Car:** Street parking can be limited near the National Mall, especially during peak season. Consider using public transportation, ride-sharing services, or biking if possible.

GPS Coordinates: 14th St & Constitution Ave NW, Washington, DC 20004 (38° 53′ 42″ N, 77° 00′ 25″ W) - Entrance near the Washington Monument

Permit/Pass/Fees:

- There is no entrance fee to visit the Washington Monument Grounds themselves. However, there may be fees for specific events or attractions within the grounds, such as tours of the Washington Monument itself.

Website:

- For information on the Washington Monument Grounds, the Washington Monument, and the National Mall, visit the National Park Service website: https://www.nps.gov/wamo/

Fun Facts about the Washington Monument Grounds:

- The Washington Monument, a towering 555-foot obelisk, is the tallest structure in Washington D.C. and a prominent landmark on the National Mall.

- The grassy knoll surrounding the monument was created in the 1880s to conceal the monument's foundation.

- The grounds feature a network of pedestrian walkways, monuments, and memorials, including memorials for World War II veterans and Dr. Martin Luther King Jr.

- The grounds are also known for their iconic cherry blossom trees, a spectacular sight during the National Cherry Blossom Festival in spring.

- Beyond its historical significance, the Washington Monument Grounds serve as a popular spot for picnics, leisure walks, and outdoor recreation in the heart of the nation's capital.

MUSEUM OF THE BIBLE, WASHINGTON D.C.

Standing just three blocks from the U.S. Capitol Building, the Museum of the Bible in Washington D.C. is a major museum dedicated to exploring the history, narrative, and global impact of the Bible. This impressive 430,000-square-foot museum features rare and fascinating artifacts, interactive exhibits, and educational programs for visitors of all ages and backgrounds.

400 4th St SW, Washington, DC 20024, United States - +18664306682

Closest City/Town: Washington D.C.

Best Time to Visit:

- The Museum of the Bible is open year-round, except for January 1, Thanksgiving, and December 25.

- Consider visiting during weekdays to avoid crowds, especially during peak tourist season.

- Spring and summer offer comfortable weather for exploring the museum and potentially the surrounding sights.

Getting Around:

- **Metro:** Take the Metro's Orange, Blue, or Silver Line to Federal Center SW station. From there, it's a short walk (about 5 minutes) to the museum.

- **Car:** Parking is available at the museum, but it can fill up on busy days. Consider using public transportation or ride-sharing services if possible.

GPS Coordinates: 400 4th St SW, Washington, DC 20024 (38° 53' 51" N, 77° 00' 22" W)

Permit/Pass/Fees:

- General admission fees apply for entrance to the Museum of the Bible. Discounted rates are available for seniors, students, and groups. You can purchase tickets online in advance or at the museum entrance: https://museumofthebible.org/tickets

Website:

- For current hours, information on exhibits, educational programs, and special events, visit the Museum of the Bible website: https://museumofthebible.org/

Fun Facts about the Museum of the Bible:

- Despite its name, the Museum of the Bible is not affiliated with any particular religion and aims to present a broad historical and cultural perspective on the Bible's influence.

- The museum's collection boasts over 40,000 artifacts, including biblical papyri, Torah scrolls, rare printed Bibles, and archaeological treasures.

- Interactive exhibits allow visitors to delve deeper into the stories and history of the Bible.

- The museum also hosts lectures, workshops, and special events throughout the year, offering opportunities for learning and engagement.

- The Museum of the Bible serves as a unique platform for exploring the enduring legacy of the Bible in society, art, culture, and history.

WATERGATE STEPS, WASHINGTON D.C.

The Watergate Steps, located along the Potomac River west of the Lincoln Memorial in Washington D.C., hold a curious place in history. Often mistakenly linked to the infamous Watergate scandal, these curved steps hold a much older story.

Ohio Dr SW, Washington, DC 20004, United States

Closest City/Town: Washington D.C. (West Potomac Park)

Best Time to Visit:

• The Watergate Steps are accessible year-round, offering a scenic spot along the Potomac River.

• Consider visiting during daylight hours for the best views and a peaceful atmosphere.

• Weekends tend to be busier than weekdays, especially during peak tourist season.

Getting Around:

- **Metro:** Take the Metro's Blue or Orange Line to Foggy Bottom station. From there, it's a moderate walk (about 15-20 minutes) or a short ride-sharing service trip to the Lincoln Memorial and the Watergate Steps.

- **Walking/Biking:** The steps are situated near the Lincoln Memorial, making them accessible on foot or by renting a bike.

- **Car:** Street parking can be limited near the National Mall, especially during peak season. Consider using public transportation, ride-sharing services, or biking if possible.

GPS Coordinates: 38° 53' 22" N, 77° 04' 00" W (West Potomac Park, Washington D.C. 20037)

Permit/Pass/Fees:

- There is no entrance fee to visit the Watergate Steps themselves.

Website:

- For information on the Lincoln Memorial, surrounding park area, and the National Mall, visit the National Park Service website: https://www.nps.gov/rocr/contacts.htm

Fun Facts about the Watergate Steps:

- Originally designed as a grand ceremonial entrance to the city for arriving dignitaries traveling by boat, the Watergate Steps never fulfilled this purpose.

- The name "Watergate" refers to the historic location, not the political scandal. "Water Gate" was a term used in the 18th century to describe a point of entry along the water.

- For a brief period in the 1930s, the steps served as a stage for floating orchestra performances, offering a unique open-air concert venue.

- Due to noise from airplanes disrupting the music, the concerts eventually stopped, and the Watergate Steps became a place for quiet contemplation and scenic river views.

- While not directly connected to the Watergate scandal, these steps offer a glimpse into Washington D.C.'s history and a reminder of the importance of accurate historical context.

PLANET WORD, WASHINGTON D.C.

Welcome to Planet Word, an immersive language experience located in the heart of Washington D.C.! Housed within the historic Franklin School building, this museum ignites a love of language through interactive exhibits, playful activities, and fascinating displays.

925 13th St NW, Washington, DC 20005, United States - +12029313139

Closest City/Town: Washington D.C.

Best Time to Visit:

• Planet Word is open daily, typically from 10:00 am to 5:00 pm.

• Consider weekdays for a potentially less crowded experience, especially during peak tourist season.

• Pay attention to special events or programs that may interest you and plan your visit accordingly.

Details on Getting Around:

- **Metro:** Take the Metro's Yellow or Blue Line to Smithsonian station. From there, it's a short walk (about 10 minutes south) to the Franklin School and Planet Word.

- **Walking/Biking:** Planet Word is situated on the National Mall, making it easily accessible on foot or by renting a bike.

- **Car:** Street parking can be limited, especially near the National Mall during peak season. Consider using public transportation, ride-sharing services, or biking if possible.

GPS Coordinate: Enid A. Haupt Garden: 750 Independence Ave SW, Washington, DC 20560 (38° 53′ 19″ N, 77° 00′ 27″ W) - Planet Word is located within the garden.

Permit/Pass/Fees:

- While there is no entrance fee to the Enid A. Haupt Garden, there is a general admission fee to enter Planet Word itself. Discounted rates are available for children, seniors, and groups. You can purchase tickets online in advance or at the museum entrance: https://planetwordmuseum.org/

Website:

- For information on current hours, exhibits, educational programs, and special events, visit the Planet Word website: https://planetwordmuseum.org/

Fun Facts about Planet Word:

- Inspired by the Temple of Heaven in Beijing, China, Planet Word features a unique design that reflects the importance of communication and language across cultures.

- Interactive exhibits allow visitors to explore the history of language, the science of communication, and the power of words in storytelling and creative expression.

- Planet Word even boasts a "talking wall" where visitors can converse with language ambassadors from around the world!

- The museum caters to all ages, offering engaging experiences for children, adults, and language enthusiasts of all backgrounds.

- Planet Word serves as a vibrant space to celebrate the power of language, encouraging exploration, learning, and a deeper appreciation for the magic of words.

WASHINGTON TRAVEL JOURNAL

Date: _____ Transport: _____

Weather	☁ ☀ 💧 🌙 ❄

Checklist For This Trip

_____
_____
_____
_____
_____
_____
_____
_____
_____
_____
_____
_____
_____
_____

Places:

Notes

Special Memories

_____
_____
_____
_____

ANACOSTIA COMMUNITY MUSEUM, WASHINGTON D.C.

Standing proudly in the Anacostia neighborhood of Washington D.C., the Anacostia Community Museum serves as a vital institution dedicated to preserving and showcasing the social and cultural history of urban communities. This Smithsonian museum, the first federally funded community museum in the United States, offers a platform for local voices and stories often overlooked in traditional historical narratives.

1901 Fort Pl SE, Washington, DC 20020, United States - +12026334820

Closest City/Town: Washington D.C. (Anacostia neighborhood)

Best Time to Visit:

• The museum is open daily from 10:00 am to 5:00 pm.

• Weekdays tend to be less crowded than weekends, especially during peak tourist season.

• Consider attending a special event or program for an enriched museum experience (check the website for schedules).

• Guided tours provide insightful information about the exhibits and the museum's mission.

Details on Getting Around:

• **Metro:** Take the Metro's Green Line to Anacostia station. The museum is located about a mile from the station, so you can either walk (approximately 20 minutes) or use a ride-sharing service.

• **Bus:** Several Metrobus lines stop near the museum.

• **Car:** Free on-site parking is available, though it can fill up on busy days. Consider using public transportation or ride-sharing services if possible.

GPS Coordinates: 1901 Fort Place SE, Washington, DC 20003 (38° 50′ 43″ N, 76° 55′ 48″ W)

Permit/Pass/Fees:

• There is no entrance fee to visit the Anacostia Community Museum itself. Donations are gratefully accepted to support the museum's mission.

Website:

- For information on current exhibits, educational programs, events, and the museum's history, visit the official website: https://anacostia.si.edu/

Fun Facts about the Anacostia Community Museum:

- Founded in 1967, the museum emerged from a desire to bring the Smithsonian Institution's vast resources closer to the Anacostia neighborhood and empower local residents to share their stories.

- The museum's collection features artifacts, photographs, and documents that illuminate the experiences of African Americans and other communities in Washington D.C.

- Exhibits explore themes of social justice, urban renewal, education, and cultural identity.

- The Anacostia Community Museum actively engages with the community through workshops, lectures, and public programs, fostering dialogue and cultural understanding.

- As a space for community voices and narratives, the Anacostia Community Museum serves as a powerful testament to the richness and resilience of urban communities.

THE EXORCIST STEPS, WASHINGTON D.C.

For fans of the iconic 1973 horror film "The Exorcist," a trip to Washington D.C. wouldn't be complete without a visit to the Exorcist Steps. These Georgetown steps, officially known as the 36th Street Steps, gained fame as the setting for a pivotal scene in the movie.

Washington, DC 20007, United States.

Closest City/Town: Washington D.C. (Georgetown neighborhood)

Best Time to Visit:

• The steps are accessible any time of day, year-round.

• Consider visiting during daylight hours for better visibility and to avoid potentially crowded sidewalks, especially on weekends.

• If you're interested in the history of the Georgetown neighborhood or the filming of "The Exorcist," a guided walking tour can offer additional insights.

Details on Getting Around:

- **Metro:** Take the Metro's Blue or Orange Line to Georgetown Waterfront station. From there, it's a short walk (about 10 minutes north) to M Street and the Exorcist Steps.

- **Walking/Biking:** The steps are situated in the heart of Georgetown, making them easily accessible on foot or by renting a bike.

- **Car:** Street parking can be limited, especially on weekends and during peak tourist season. Consider using public transportation, ride-sharing services, or biking if possible.

GPS Coordinates: 38° 53′ 51″ N, 77° 00′ 27″ W (M Street NW between 35th & 36th Streets, Washington, DC)

Permit/Pass/Fees:

- There is no entrance fee or permit required to visit the Exorcist Steps themselves.

Website:

- While there's no website dedicated solely to the steps, several websites provide interesting information on the filming locations of "The Exorcist" in Georgetown, including the steps:

  o https://www.atlasobscura.com/places/the-exorcist-stairs-washington-dc

Fun Facts about the Exorcist Steps:

- The steps, built in 1895, were originally constructed as a fire escape and shortcut between Prospect Street and Canal Road.

- In "The Exorcist," the scene filmed on the steps depicts a possessed Regan MacNeil (played by Linda Blair) tumbling down the stairs. In reality, a stunt double with padding performed the fall.

- The steps have become a popular tourist destination for horror movie fans, with some visitors attempting to recreate the iconic scene from the film.

- The Exorcist Steps are just one location in Georgetown featured in the movie. Other recognizable spots include Georgetown University and Carnaby Street.

- Whether you're a horror buff or simply curious about a piece of cinematic history, the Exorcist Steps offer a glimpse into Georgetown's past and its unexpected Hollywood connection.

NATIONAL MUSEUM OF THE UNITED STATES NAVY, WASHINGTON D.C.

The National Museum of the United States Navy, often referred to as the Navy Museum, is the flagship museum for the U.S. Navy. Located in Washington D.C. on the grounds of the Washington Navy Yard, this museum chronicles the rich history of the American Navy from its 18th-century beginnings to the present day.

736 Sicard St SE, Washington, DC 20374, United States - +12026850589

Closest City/Town: Washington D.C. (Washington Navy Yard)

Best Time to Visit:

- The Navy Museum is open to the public Tuesday through Saturday, from 9:00 am to 4:00 pm.

- Weekdays tend to be less crowded than weekends, especially during peak tourist season.

- Consider attending a special program or guided tour for a richer museum experience (check the website for schedules).

Details on Getting Around:

- **Metro:** Take the Metro's Green Line to Navy Yard station. **However, be aware** that due to security measures, visitors cannot enter the Navy Yard directly from the Metro station.

- After exiting the Navy Yard station, call the museum (202-685-0589) for an escort, or use a ride-sharing service like Uber or Lyft to reach the museum entrance at 11th and O Streets SE.

- **Car:** Limited public parking is available on-site for a fee. Street parking can be limited, especially during peak season. Consider using public transportation or ride-sharing services if possible.

GPS Coordinates: 748 Washington Ave SE, Washington, DC 20003 (38° 50′ 52″ N, 77° 00′ 13″ W)

Permit/Pass/Fees:

- There is no entrance fee to visit the National Museum of the United States Navy. However, there may be fees for specific programs or events.

Website:

- For information on current exhibits, educational programs, tours, and the museum's collections, visit the official website: https://www.history.navy.mil/content/history/museums/nmusn.html

Fun Facts about the National Museum of the United States Navy:

- Established in 1961, the Navy Museum boasts an impressive collection of artifacts, including ship models, weapons, uniforms, and personal belongings of notable naval figures.

- A centerpiece of the museum is the USS Constitution's fighting top, a lookout platform used during the War of 1812.

- The museum features permanent and temporary exhibits that explore various aspects of naval history, from battles and technological advancements to social issues and humanitarian efforts.

- Visitors can delve deeper into the stories behind the artifacts through interactive displays and multimedia presentations.

- The National Museum of the United States Navy serves as a valuable resource for learning about the Navy's role in shaping American history and its ongoing global impact.

FRANCISCAN MONASTERY OF THE HOLY LAND IN AMERICA, WASHINGTON D.C.

Situated on Mount Saint Sepulcher in the Brookland neighborhood of Washington D.C., the Franciscan Monastery of the Holy Land in America offers a unique blend of history, culture, and spiritual refuge. This Franciscan complex features a beautiful church, serene gardens, and replicas of shrines from the Holy Land, providing a captivating glimpse into the land central to Christianity.

1400 Quincy St NE, Washington, DC 20017, United States - +12025266800

Closest City/Town: Washington D.C. (Brookland neighborhood)

Best Time to Visit:

• The Monastery grounds are open daily from 9:30 am to 5:00 pm.

• The church itself observes specific hours for prayer and services (check the website for details).

• Consider visiting during weekdays for a potentially less crowded experience, especially during peak tourist season.

• Docent-led tours are offered on Saturdays, providing insightful information about the Monastery's history and collections.

Details on Getting Around:

• **Metro:** Take the Metro's Red Line to Brookland-CUA station. From there, it's a short walk (about 10 minutes east) to the Monastery.

• **Bus:** Several Metrobus lines stop near the Monastery.

• **Car:** Street parking can be limited, especially during peak season. Consider using public transportation or ride-sharing services if possible.

GPS Coordinates: 1400 Quincy St. NE, Washington, DC 20017 (38° 54' 59" N, 77° 01' 33" W)

Permit/Pass/Fees:

• The Monastery grounds and gardens are free to explore.

• There is an admission fee for guided tours of the Monastery itself. Donations are gratefully accepted for the upkeep of the Monastery.

Website:

• For information on hours, tours, events, and the Monastery's history, visit their website: https://myfranciscan.org/

Fun Facts about the Franciscan Monastery of the Holy Land in America:

• Founded in 1899, the Monastery is a unique haven inspired by the Holy Land.

- The centerpiece of the Monastery church is a replica of the grotto believed to be the birthplace of Jesus in Bethlehem.

- Visitors can stroll through serene meditation gardens featuring over 1,000 rose bushes and a replica of the Catacombs of Rome.

- The Monastery serves as a center for interfaith dialogue and cultural understanding.

- Beyond its religious significance, the Franciscan Monastery offers a peaceful retreat from the bustle of the city, inviting exploration, reflection, and a touch of the Holy Land right in Washington D.C.

Washington Travel Journal

Date: .... Transport: ....

Weather	☁ ☀ 💧 🌙 ❄

Checklist For This Trip

Places:

Special Memories

Notes

WASHINGTON TRAVEL JOURNAL

Date: .... Transport: ....

Weather

Checklist For This Trip

Places:

Notes

Special Memories

WASHINGTON TRAVEL JOURNAL

Date: _____ Transport: _____

Weather

Checklist For This Trip

Places:

Notes

Special Memories

WASHINGTON TRAVEL JOURNAL

Date: _____ Transport: _____

Weather	

Checklist For This Trip

_____
_____
_____
_____
_____
_____
_____
_____
_____
_____
_____
_____
_____

Special Memories

_____
_____
_____
_____

Places:

_____
_____
_____
_____
_____
_____

Notes

t

Made in United States
Troutdale, OR
12/27/2024

27253484R00075